BEAD PLAY
every day

20+ Projects with Peyote, Herringbone & More

Beth Stone

KALMBACH BOOKS

WAUKESHA, WI

To my loving and supportive husband, Sheldon, who needs more sports memorabilia almost as much as I need more beads.

Kalmbach Books
21027 Crossroads Circle
Waukesha, Wisconsin 53186
www.JewelryAndBeadingStore.com

Published in 2015
19 18 17 16 15   1 2 3 4 5

Manufactured in China

ISBN: 978-1-62700-081-9
EISBN: 978-1-62700-082-6

Editor: Karin Van Voorhees
Book Design: Lisa Schroeder
Photographer: William Zuback

Library of Congress Control Number: 2015930763

CONTENTS

i ♥ beaDs!

Beads and design ideas swirl through my head every day. I wake up designing, and I go to sleep designing. I am a lifelong beader, descended from beaders, and my passion goes beyond what anyone might perceive as *normal*. My beads go with me wherever I go.

I love beads! I love to look at them, touch them, stitch them together, create new thread paths, and watch structures appear before my eyes. It simply makes me feel good to share everything I know. So here goes:

This book, my third, is for the beader who has a good working knowledge of basic stitches such as peyote and herringbone and also how to create stitched ropes. This book is for beaders with a growing interest in adding techniques and variations to their repertoire. As always, I will continue to be your cheerleader as you take what I teach in a new and unique direction.

The techniques in this book are all born from several basic rope stitches. They can be used alone or in combinations, and you'll see examples throughout the book. While the order corresponds with my sample rope, it is not necessary for you to work or learn in that order. There are detailed instructions for each technique/variation, and each technique has a name for easy reference. It is my goal to give you the tools and encouragement needed to become the architect of unique designs.

This book has been a challenge, but also a reward. Like so many other bead artists and designers, I am seeking a new thread path, an original design, and perhaps a new technique to help you create your own beautiful innovations so you can love beading as much as I do.

Yes, I love beads, and I know I am not the only one. But my passion is genuine and I have a desire to share what I know so you can benefit from the countless hours I've put into this craft. Each piece in this book evolved from something else. After doing this for so long, I am always amazed when I discover something new. And when I do, I must share it!

The energy in my bead brain, which for me never turns off, is like the energy of a roulette wheel that has a little ball rolling around and around, past number after number, before finally settling into just one spot. This is why *Bead Play Every Day* is more than just a title; it represents who I am as a beader and an artist because I like to play with beads every day in some way, shape, or form. I also like to just sit with them and let them *speak to me*. Each time I sit down to bead, multiple ideas swirl around. If I am just a little bit patient, my head and hands will settle on a design or a thread path or a color scheme that will take me to yet another level of my beading evolution. It's a game I love to play.

Where do I find my ideas and inspirations? Architecture and color and nature are my go-to places. I also love to look at metalwork and microscopic images. When I get a chill or feel butterflies in my stomach, I know I have been inspired. I try to not look at beadwork by other artists because I don't want an idea or someone else's design to get stuck in my head.

This book began with the idea of creating one long three-dimensional structural rope, and highlighting numerous techniques along the rope that could be used for individual projects. As I worked to create new techniques and variations, I found myself wandering over to flat, two-dimensional techniques. This allowed me to use some of the new beads that have recently come onto the market. I have found

through trial and error that not all beads work in all types of dimensional designs—some beads are better suited for flat projects and some work with any type of project. That said, you are welcome to use any beads available for any project. It's all about combining play and experimentation with trial and error. I learn so much more from my mistakes than anything else.

I love to tell stories about my bead journey. Sometimes the stories relate to the technique or project and sometimes they don't. My lack of focus is both a gift and a curse. Like the dog darts after a squirrel, my "squirrel" is a new idea that pops into my head, and I have to stop whatever I am doing and bring the idea to life.

I am not a complicated beader. I like to teach simple techniques that are easy to see and photograph. My step-by-step photos are in primary colors to make the teaching easier. Most of my finished work is in palettes of muted and shiny earth tones. I hope to share my ideas so you can take them to a different place and make them your own! Every technique and design presented will look very different with various colors or patterns. Choose what *you* love and have fun experimenting.

When I look at my ever-growing bead collection, I know that hiding in there somewhere is something new waiting to be discovered—whether it's a new color, size combination, or something else. I never know what's going to appear and am either happily surprised or surprisingly frustrated, depending on the day. I enjoy the frustrating part most of all because it gives me a chance to use my inborn engineering and math skills to test my design and structural abilities. Once I figure something out, I like to share it with anyone who is interested.

I believe that the secret to creativity is knowing where to find your sources. The work of my friend, Marlene Quigley,

> *The meaning of life is to find your gift. The purpose of life is to give it away.*
> *-Pablo Picasso*

was a major source of inspiration for this book. She helped me continue a bead journey I had recently begun using multiple techniques in one continuous rope. More of this story can be found on p. 14. I thank Marlene for throwing her work at me as if to say, "here, do something with this," and for years of love and encouragement.

Throughout this book there are 20 complete projects, and while I hope you will try them, my real wish is that this book finds a home in the libraries of beaders everywhere. I want my work to spark a new flame for new works of wearable art. If you discover a new technique or variation along the way, then I have done my job.

I've skipped a lot of introductory basics because you are already an experienced beader with a good working knowledge of many of the basic seed bead stitches (peyote, herringbone, brick). You know all about threads and needles and your personal preference for using thread conditioner or not. You know that beads come in a wide variety of shapes, sizes, colors and finishes, and you know that the process of inventing new bead shapes, colors, and finishes is never ending. You don't need me to help with that.

Why do I want to give away all of my secrets? Quite simply, I believe that if artists don't share their work, techniques, and enthusiasm, the art will die. If we, a world-wide collective of bead artists, authors, designers, innovators and lovers of beads, stopped sharing what we know, the art, like unused languages, will slowly and naturally fade away. And that would be sad, so I simply and happily do my part to perpetuate the art.

Welcome to Bead Play Every Day!

Let's Play!

TERMINOLOGY & OTHER THINGS TO KNOW

STEP-UP

One term I use very often throughout this book is step-up. The projects presented in this book are rope techniques that require working in the round. Imagine building a tall, tall building with each "round" or "row" of beads as a new floor. As each floor is constructed, notice that as the last bead is added in the round, there will be an additional bead to pass up through. This additional bead is the first bead of the new "floor" just created. The action of passing up through this bead is called a step-up. Using the illustration below as an example of this technique, beads 1, 2, and 3 comprise the first round. Beads 4–9 comprise the second round. The last stitch in this second round is secured by passing through bead 1. To "step-up," pass through the first bead in the 4–9 round, which is bead 4.

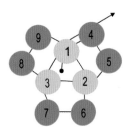

When working with pairs of beads (i.e. tubular herringbone) there are times when the directions state to add a bead **within** a pair or **between** a pair. In the illustration here, the square beads are added **within** pairs of beads and the triangle beads are added **between** pairs of beads. At some points, directions will be given to add beads between "each" bead. In these cases, a bead will be added between every bead in the row.

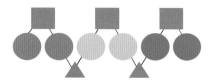

THREAD

Every beader has a personal preference when it comes to thread choice. Finding the one that works best may be a matter of trial and error. Some of the most popular threads are: Fireline, Nymo D, Silamide, C-Lon, SoNO, Wildfire, One-G, and Power Pro. My personal favorite changes often and today it is black One-G on the large spool.

Fireline has a coating on it that can rub off on light colored beads. I suggest running the Fireline through a baby wipe or dryer sheet to remove as much of this residue as possible.

tip!

Pam's Bead Garden in Farmington, Michigan, gave me a great thread tip, although I am not sure where they got it. Cut a length of Nymo from a large spool of Nymo D (it's actually a bit thicker than the Nymo D on the tiny spool) and pull it gently through a heated straightening iron. This somehow strengthens it, but be careful not to stop while pulling the thread through the iron because the heat will cut the thread. (I learned this quickly all on my own.)

tip!

Fireline and Power Pro can be found in the fishing department of large sporting goods stores.

BEADS

Seed beads come in a wide variety of sizes, shapes, colors, and finishes. Using different beads will add texture and excitement to your beadwork. Don't be afraid to experiment. My mantra —PLAY!

Some of the beads I love to use are: 11º seed beads, 8º seed beads, 6º seed beads, Delicas, triangles in all sizes, magatamas, long magatamas, cubes in all sizes, drops (long and short), hexes in all sizes, cut beads, Charlottes, Tilas, half Tilas, Twins, SuperDuos, SuperUnos, CheckMates, cupped "piggy beads," peanuts, bricks, Rullas, Rizos, two-hole triangles, and O-beads.

Beads also come in a wide variety of finishes from matte to metallic, pearlized to Picasso, and many more in between, including the new baroque finish. Right now I may have a favorite bead and new color combination, but I know that will change as soon as something new catches my eye.

Scattered throughout this book are a few other beads such as top-drilled pearls, fire-polished faceted Czech beads, daggers, large glass drops and more, which are used for accent.

As for bead size, 15º, 11º, 8º, and 6º are the most popular, with the larger number correlating to the smaller bead.

bead tip!

Having trouble threading the needle? Try "needling your thread." Push the needle onto the thread instead of trying to push the thread into the eye of the needle. Did you know the eye of a needle has two different sides? The eye is wider on one side than the other. Try turning the needle over and see if the thread slides in easier. Yes, I have a brain full of this type of stuff.

Tubular Stitch Tutorials

All of the tubular stitches in this book are based on one of four basic stitches: tubular peyote, tubular herringbone, skinny tubular herringbone, and a stitch I call the diamond stitch. Also, all of the techniques presented are built on a base of either three or four beads. Some techniques can be done using either base number and some techniques can ONLY be done using one of these bases. As each technique and variation is presented, the necessary base will be indicated.

NOTE: If you feel inspired, try some of the techniques using different base-bead numbers—six, eight, or more. Play!

A great way to understand the construction of a beaded rope is to envision the construction of a skyscraper with the first round of beads as the first floor and each round of beads, the subsequent floors, built one on top of the other. While learning and mastering the four basic rope stitch techniques, it is important to note that the illustrations are drawn flat to show proper bead placement. The beads will actually be pulled gently into a tube shape as the stitching progresses. The visible "threads" in the drawings and step-by-step photos will not be visible in the actual work.

TUBULAR PEYOTE

Tubular peyote can be worked from a three- or four-bead base, but for the purpose of illustration, this is a three-bead base.

1 Pick up three beads and sew through the first bead again to create a circle **a**.

2 Using peyote stitch, add one bead between each of the beads in the previous round **b**.

3 To position for the next round, step-up by passing through the first bead added in this round **c**.

4 Add one bead between each of the three beads added in the previous round. Remember to pull the beads into the beginning of a tube shape. When looking at the beadwork from the side, this round will lie directly on top of the beads from the base row **d**.

5 To position for the next round, step-up by passing through the first bead added in this round **e**.

Remember that this is a peyote stitch. Each round of beads is offset from the previous round. Rows 1, 3, 5, 7, etc. will lie on top of each other and rows 2, 4, 6, 8, etc. will lie on top of each other **f**.

Continue until you reach your desired length.

*tubular
peyote*

a

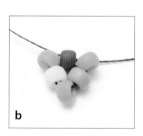

b

c

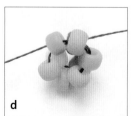

d

e

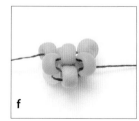

f

tubular
herringbone

TUBULAR HERRINGBONE

1 Pick up six beads and create a circle. Treat these beads as three pairs. Note that the working thread is on the left **a**.

2 Pick up two beads, and pass through the second bead of the first pair, and through the first bead of the second pair. Note that the working thread is on the left **b**.

3 Pick up two beads, and pass through the second bead of the second pair, and up through the first bead of the third pair. Note the working thread is on the bottom **c**.

4 Pick up two beads, and pass through the second bead of the third pair and the first bead of the first pair **d**. Notice that the working thread is on the top.

5 Pass through the first bead added in this round to step-up **e**. Note that the working thread is on the top.

6 With the thread exiting the first bead of a pair, pick up two beads, and pass through the second bead of a pair and immediately through the first bead of the next pair **f**. Repeat two more times.

7 Step-up into the first bead of the first pair of beads added in this round **g**. Pulling the beadwork gently will create the tube shape. The threads that were visible between the bead pairs will disappear **h**, **i**.

a

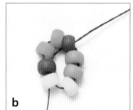

b

c

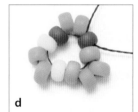

d

e

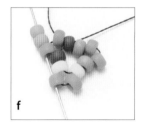

f

g

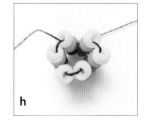

h

i

TUBULAR SKINNY HERRINGBONE

NOTE: Tubular skinny herringbone can only be created with a four-bead base.

1 Pick up four beads and create a circle as shown. Treat these beads as two pairs. The working thread is on the left coming out of the orange bead **a**.

2 Pick up two beads. Pass through the second bead of the first pair and through the first bead of the second pair. The working thread is on the bottom exiting the green bead **b**.

3 Pick up two beads. Pass through the second bead of the second pair **c**. The working thread is exiting the green bead.

4 To finish the stitch, pass through the first bead of the base pair, and to position for the next round, pass through the first bead of the first pair added in this round **d**. The working thread is exiting the blue bead.

5 Pick up two beads. Pass through the next three beads. Pick up two beads. Pass through the next three beads **e**. Gently pull the beads into a tube shape.

   It is important to note that you are creating a bead tube. The bead pairs from steps 2 and 3 will actually be sitting on top of the bead pairs from step 1. The bead pairs from step 5 will be sitting on top of the bead pairs from steps 2 and 3.

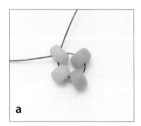

a

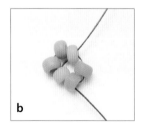

b

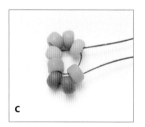

c

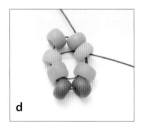

d

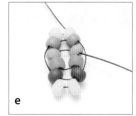

e

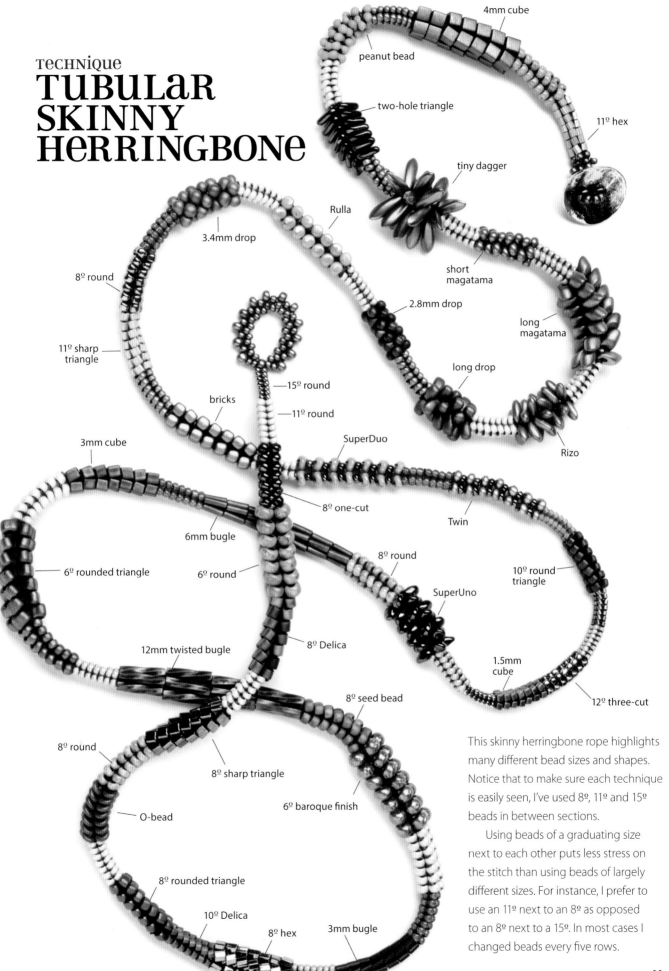

TECHNIQUE
TUBULAR SKINNY HERRINGBONE

4mm cube

peanut bead

two-hole triangle

11º hex

tiny dagger

Rulla

3.4mm drop

short magatama

8º round

2.8mm drop

long magatama

11º sharp triangle

long drop

15º round

bricks

11º round

SuperDuo

Rizo

3mm cube

8º one-cut

Twin

6mm bugle

8º round

10º round triangle

6º rounded triangle

6º round

SuperUno

8º Delica

1.5mm cube

12mm twisted bugle

12º three-cut

8º seed bead

8º round

8º sharp triangle

6º baroque finish

O-bead

8º rounded triangle

10º Delica

8º hex

3mm bugle

This skinny herringbone rope highlights many different bead sizes and shapes. Notice that to make sure each technique is easily seen, I've used 8º, 11º and 15º beads in between sections.

Using beads of a graduating size next to each other puts less stress on the stitch than using beads of largely different sizes. For instance, I prefer to use an 11º next to an 8º as opposed to an 8º next to a 15º. In most cases I changed beads every five rows.

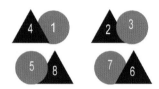

FIGURE 1

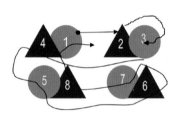

FIGURE 2

Seamless Connection

This technique is for making a seamless connection for a skinny herringbone bangle bracelet (p. 22) was first published in *More Seed Bead Stitching*. Since it hasn't changed, I am going to simply repeat it here.

Before connecting the two ends, straighten out the rope, making sure that you are connecting opposite colors to ensure a seamless finish. If not, you will need to stitch one more round. Gently pull out the first round of thread on the tail end of the rope. The beads should not fall off. Hold the two ends face to face to make sure it looks like **figure 1**. Make sure the working thread is exiting bead 1 and the tail thread is exiting bead 2. (The project on p. 22 demonstrates this technique, using bugles for bead 1 and triangles for bead 2.)

You will be starting a new stitch, but instead of picking up new beads from the bead mat, you'll use beads from the opposite end of the rope that you are attempting to connect. With the needle exiting bead 1, pass through bead 2, continue passing around through bead 3, and secure this "new" stitch by passing through bead 4.

Okay, halfway there.

Pass the needle around through bead 5, pick up bead 6, pass around through bead 7, and pass across to bead 8.

To finish the stitch, circle around back through bead 1 **figure 2**. This working thread should now be face to face with the tail thread that is exiting bead 2. Tie these two ends together, pulling gently to tighten the beadwork into the seamless connection. DO NOT tie the threads again before checking the connection. There should not be any gaps in the beadwork. If there is, or if any of the beads look out of line, undo the threads and rework the connection. Once the connection has been made correctly, tie another knot. Weave the tail thread and the working threads through the beadwork, tying little half-hitch knots along the way, and cut the thread to finish.

Seamless connections can be tricky in that you need to think backwards. If all else fails, try not to scream. Just use a button and loop or another type of closure.

DIAMOND STITCH

Diamond stitch is a tubular peyote/tubular herringbone combination. I "discovered" it a few years ago and named it this because of the way it looks from the side of the rope.

1 Pick up three beads and form a circle as shown. The working thread is on the left and the tail is on the right **a**.

2 Pick up two beads and pass through the next bead. The working thread is on the bottom and the tail is on the right **b**.

3 Pick up two beads and pass through the next bead. The working thread is on the bottom and the tail is on the top **c**.

4 Pick up two beads and pass through the first bead. To position for the next round, step-up into the fourth bead. The working thread is now exiting the blue bead on the left and the tail is on the right **d**.

Notice that there are now three pairs of beads.

5 With the thread exiting the first bead of the first pair, pick up one bead **e** and immediately pass down into the second bead of the first pair. To begin the next stitch (don't pick up another bead yet), pass through the first bead of the next pair **f**. The working thread is exiting the bottom blue bead and the tail is just hanging out on the right side.

NOTE: The base beads (orange) will not be passed through again. The visible thread will not be visible once the beads are pulled into the tube shape.

6 Pick up one bead, immediately pass through the second bead of this pair, and go up through the first bead of the next pair. The working thread is on the bottom (exiting the blue bead) and the tail is on the top **g**.

7 Pick up one bead and immediately pass through the second bead of this pair. The working thread is on the left and the little lonely tail is still just hanging out on the right **h**. There is no way to photograph these steps without the tail thread "photobombing."

8 Pass through the first bead of the first pair and the first red bead to position for the next round **i**. The working thread is exiting the red bead to the left and that darn tail is still hanging out.

9 At this point, start nudging the beads into a tube shape **j**, **k**.

10 The only beads used for the next round are the red beads in the photos. Add two beads between each red bead **l**. Step-up.

11 Repeat steps 5–7, adding two beads between each of the beads from the previous round. Step-up. Continue alternating one and two beads per round **m**. Here is the rope viewed from the side **n**.

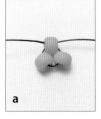

a

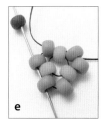

b

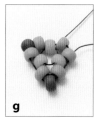

c

d

e

f

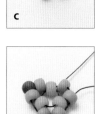

g

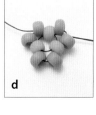

h

i

j

k

l

m

n

Bead, Play, & Love

"It is a happy talent to know how to play." Ralph Waldo Emerson

An Idea Is Born

Several years ago, I picked up a needle, thread, and some beads and started making what I hoped would be a necklace. The design was not planned, which is not unusual for me, but I knew that I wanted to create some type of rope. I began with a short section of tubular peyote and after a few rows (i. e. when boredom set in), I switched techniques and beads. As I worked, I continued to changed techniques and beads every several rows. Some of the techniques were known to me and some I just made up as I went along. As I incorporated more and more types of beads into more and more techniques, I fell madly in love with the concept. And when I completed this necklace, I knew I had stumbled upon a new signature style. I named the necklace Bead, Play, Love.

I wanted to share it. Immediately. So I did. And I was asked to teach it. GULP!

I decided that the best teaching approach would be to break the rope down into sections, so students could focus on what appealed to them and create their own unique work of art. After all, if I don't know where my creativity will take me, how can I possibly know where your creativity will take you?

The other part of this journey has to do with a fabulous gift from my friend Marlene Quigley—a bracelet using a wire technique called Viking Knit. As soon as I saw it I knew I had to recreate it in seed beads.

The bracelet led me to modify my rope necklace into Bead, Play, Love 2. This little exercise was a breakthrough for me because the mock "Viking Knit" portion (skinny herringbone) was a perfect frame to set off the faux beads, in other words, my "big ideas," without having them bump into each other like they do in the original Bead, Play, Love.

Bead, Play, Love

One thing led to another (as they do in my world), and I created the rope (aptly called Bead, Play, Love 3) that ultimately became the book you're holding right now.

Bead Play Love 3 runs at the top of most of the pages of this book to show you the wonderful techniques, which are then explained on the pages below. In addition, you'll discover projects and a few challenges along the way. Love techniques? Find the part of the rope that intrigues you and that technique will be taught on that page. Prefer a project? Choose the one you like and the techniques to help you make it will be on nearby pages. You don't need to work in any particular order, but the projects toward the end of the book combine the most techniques and are more challenging than those in the beginning.

Okay, I hear my kids' voices telling me to "just stop talking!" so let's get on with it. Wait, one more thing…it's not necessary to work in any particular order and the length of each section can be any length desired. Oh, and the beads listed for any techniques shown are for the beads I used. Please use any and all beads that are pleasing. Each technique on the rope is separated by one of the basic stitches found on p. 8–11, Some techniques require a four-bead base and some techniques require a three-bead base.

It's important to know that tubular peyote and diamond stitch can be worked from either a three-bead or four-bead base technique (and even a two-bead base). Tubular herringbone (for my purposes) uses a three-bead base, which quickly becomes a six-bead base.

Now I'm done. Let's get started!

Marlene's Viking Knit bracelet

My seed bead version

Bead, Play, Love 2

PROJECT
CIRCLE GAME

Beads

11º seed beads, one color

8º seed beads, one color

1.5 or 1.8 mm cube beads, one color

NOTE: The instructions only indicate the bead size, so feel free to use any colors that are pleasing. In order for the circles to work, please use the three sizes as indicated above.

This project is a skinny herringbone variation using two different sizes of seed beads, which causes the structure to arc around itself. I use this technique quite often as a base for pendants and rings, sometimes filling the hole with large stones. Circle Game is created using seven circles, each made up of different bead sizes and shapes to create color and texture variations. Each circle is created separately and then sewn together at the end. And, because I love stitched toggle clasps, I used the end circle as the clasp with a toggle bar stitched using my Diamond Stitch technique (p. 59). This is one of only a few of my designs where the piece isn't made with one continuous thread path.

CIRCLE 1

1 Create a skinny herringbone tube using 8º seed beads for one pair and one 11º seed bead and one cube bead for the other pair. Photos **a–c** will get you started.

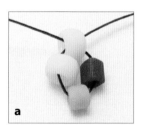

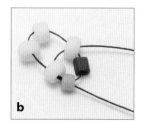

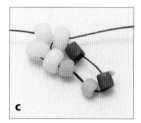

idea! **Make each circle in a different color scheme.**

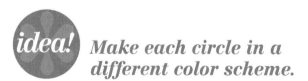

To help illustrate the seamless connection, here is another set of drawings:

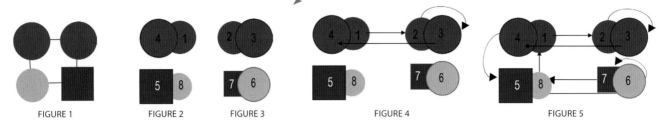

FIGURE 1　　FIGURE 2　　FIGURE 3　　FIGURE 4　　FIGURE 5

NOTE: At the end of each round make sure to pass the needle up through two beads in the stack.

2 Continue working in skinny herringbone until you have completed 28 rows. The number of rows must be even. Feel free to make yours bigger or smaller. Continue beading **d**.

3 Using the Seamless Connection instructions (above), connect the two ends, and weave in the tail and working threads, but DO NOT cut the threads **e**. The working thread will be used to embellish the circle and the tail thread may be needed to join this circle to the next one.

EMBELLISHING THE CIRCLE
Two more rounds of beads will be added to the outside of the circle.

ROUND 1
The side of the circle will looks like **f**:

Using the longest thread, weave through the beads until the thread is exiting one of the 8º beads **g**:

Pick up one cube bead and pass your needle into bead which is diagonal to the bead the thread is exiting **h**.

Pick up one 11º and pass through the next bead on the diagonal **i**.

Pick up one cube bead and pass through the next diagonal bead **j**.

Continue alternating beads until this first round of embellishment beads have circled the ring, ending with an 11º. This is the reason you need an even number of rows in the base circle. The thread will exit a cube bead.

The next round will further embellish the circle.

ROUND 2
The circle should now look like **k**:

With the thread exiting out of the cube bead, pick up one 8º and pass through the 11º which is a tiny bit diagonal to the cube bead **l**.

With the thread exiting out of the 11º, pick up one 8º and pass through the cube bead which is a tiny bit diagonal to the 11º **m**.

Continue in this manner until this round of embellishment is complete **n**. If the working thread is about 12 in. or longer, don't weave it in yet.

The first circle is complete.

 d

 e

 f

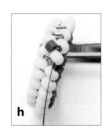 g

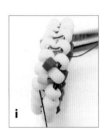 h

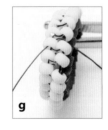 i

 j

 k

 l

 m

 n

FIGURE 6

Things to know

The next six circles are done just like this one, with some changes. I'll give you the "pattern" for each one, but feel free to experiment and play with designs and beads, as long as the beads are two different sizes to allow the arc to naturally form.

CIRCLE 2

BASE CIRCLE:
Using the directions for circle 1 as a guide, substitute cube beads for the 8ºs and use all 11ºs for the cube beads and 11ºs for 30 rows.
OUTER RING 1: 11ºs.
OUTER RING 2: 8ºs.
This circle has three rings.
OUTER RING 3: Cube beads.

CIRCLE 3

BASE CIRCLE:
Using the directions for circle 1 as a guide, use 8ºs and 11ºs for 17 rows. Alternate 11ºs and cube beads for 17 rows.
OUTER RING 1:
On top of the solid 8º section, alternate cube and 11ºs. On top of the cube and 11º section, use 8ºs.
OUTER RING 2:
On top of the alternating cube and 11º section, once again, alternate cube and 11ºs. For the 8º section, use 8ºs.

CIRCLE 4

BASE CIRCLE:
Using the instructions for circle 1 as a guide, substitute cube beads for the 8ºs and use one color of 11ºs for the 11º and cube beads for 26 rows.
OUTER RING 1: 11ºs.
OUTER RING 2: 8ºs.

CIRCLE 5

BASE CIRCLE: 8º and 11ºs for 18 rows.
OUTER CIRCLE 1: 11ºs.
OUTER RING 2: Cube beads.

CIRCLE 6

BASE CIRCLE: 11ºs and cube beads for 34 rows
OUTER CIRCLE 1: 11ºs.
OUTER CIRCLE 2: 8ºs.

CIRCLE 7

BASE CIRCLE: Cube beads and 8ºs for 36 rows.
OUTER CIRCLE 1: Cube beads.
OUTER CIRCLE 2: 11ºs.
Learn the technique, change it, mix it, and play with it until it becomes yours!
Use diamond stitch (p. 59) or another stitch to create a toggle bar.

beaDS

Beads

11º seed beads

8º seed beads

10–12 10mm round beads or gemstones

tecHNique
WaVY SKINNY HeRRINGBONe

This technique is a variation of the circles described in the previous project and shown at the end of the rope. To create the wavy form, the positions of the beads are reversed every 10 rows. I like to challenge myself to create my work in one continuous thread path and therefore, the large stones are added as the piece is stitched.

1 Begin on a four-bead base. Work skinny herringbone for 10 rows using the two different sized beads; one size for each pair. The piece will begin to naturally arc. The working thread is on the left and the tail thread is on the right **a**.

2 Pick up one accent bead (pick a bead size that nestles nicely into the curve). Pass through the 11º seed bead directly across from the 11º the thread is exiting. Make a U-turn, passing through the second 11º of the same first pair, as shown. The tail thread is on the right **b**.

3 Pass back through the accent bead. Tighten the accent bead into place. The working thread is on the left and exiting the 11º that is in the foreground **c**.

4 Work 10 more rows of skinny herringbone making sure to begin with a pair of 8º seed beads. The beads will arc in the opposite direction. The working thread will be exiting the first bead of an 8º pair **d**.

a

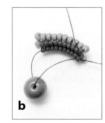
b

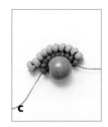
c

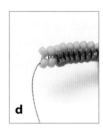
d

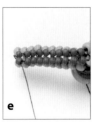
e

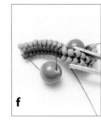
f

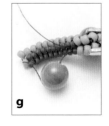
g

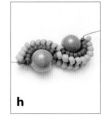
h

20

5 To position for the addition of the next accent bead, it is necessary to pass down into the first 11º of the 11º pair **e**.

6 Pick up an accent bead. Pass the thread into the 11º directly across from the 11º the thread is exiting. The thread is passed through the end 11º ONLY. I moved the working thread out of the way for the photo. The thread is NOT exiting out of one of the 8ºs **f**.

7 Make a U-turn and pass through the second 11º of the end 11º pair **g**.

8 Pass back through the accent bead.

9 Pass through the 11º that was the NOT the exit bead prior to adding the accent bead (the 11º in the foreground in this picture) **h**. Tighten the accent bead into place.

10 Stitch 10 rows of skinny herringbone, beginning with the 8ºs. Continue working this pattern until you reach the desired length for a bracelet or necklace.

Custom toggle clasp

These clasps are made from a skinny herringbone loop and a fan toggle. To make the loop, I stitched 24 rows of skinny herringbone, allowed it to curve, and secured the loop to the main body of the bracelet. Instructions for the fan technique are on p. 27. Between the body of the bracelet and the fan toggle, I added a short section of "herringbone with a flair" (shown here) to give the toggle some flexibility (it helps prevent breaking from overuse). Use 11º seed beads; three colors are used here for teaching purposes.

1 Pick up two 11º seed beads. Pass the needle back through the first bead so the working thread and tail thread are exiting it in opposite directions **a**.
2 Pick up two 11ºs. Pass the needle back down through the second bead from the first row **b**.
3 Pick up one 11º and pass the needle up through the second bead in the top row. This positions you to begin the next row **c**.
4 Pick up two 11ºs. Pass the needle down into the first bead from the previous row **d**.
5 Pick up one 11º and pass the needle up through the second bead on the top row **e**. Now begin the fan toggle.

PROJECT
BUGLE & TRIANGLE
BANGLE BRACELET

Beads

5mm bugle beads
10º triangle beads

Practice the skinny herringbone technique with this great little project. Using the skinny herringbone instructions (p. 10), use two triangle beads and one bugle bead for each stitch, as follows:

1 Pick up two triangle beads, one bugle bead, two triangles, and one bugle. Treat the two triangles as one bead. Pass through the first two triangles to create a circle. The working thread is on the left and the tail thread is on the right **a**.

2 Pick up one bugle and two triangles. Pass through the base bugle and two triangles. The working thread is exiting the bottom triangles and the tail thread is off to the right **b**.

3 Pick up one bugle and two triangles. Pass through the base bugle and the two base triangles. Step-up into the bugle added in step 2 to position for the next round. The working thread is at the top and the tail thread is still just hanging out on the right **c**.

4 Pick up two triangles and one bugle. Pass down the two triangles and skip over the bases. Pass up into the end bugle. The thread loop shown will not be visible once the work is pulled into a tube. The working thread is at the bottom and the tail thread is on the right **d**.

5 Pick up two triangles and one bugle. Pass through the two triangles, skip over the bases, and pass through the bugle. Step-up through the two triangles to position for the next round. The working thread is at the top and the tail thread is on the right **e**. The thread loop on the right will not be visible once the beads are pulled into the rope shape.

6 Gently pull the beads into the rope shape **f**.

To continue, add beads for each row, noting that if the thread is exiting a bugle, the stitch will begin with two triangles and vice versa.

To finish this bracelet as a bangle, follow the seamless connection instructions (p. 12). Or, simply finish the bracelet with any type of clasp.

a

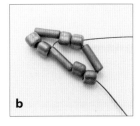

b

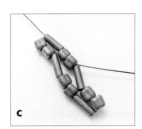

c

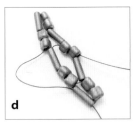

d

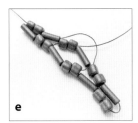

e

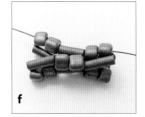

f

harlequin diamond

offset harlequin diamond

Beads

11º seed beads in one or two colors

drop beads (optional)

TECHNIQUE
HARLEQUIN DIAMOND

This diamond technique is another variation of skinny tubular herringbone using increases and decreases.

This technique incorporates the elements of peyote along each side with the two-bead element of herringbone on each short edge. This technique has a front and back, which allows for different colors to be used for each side. Or not.

You need to create a two-bead base (described below) before you can begin this technique, which is built on a skinny herringbone base.

1 With the thread exiting out of the first bead of the first pair, pick up one bead (red in this process shot) and pass down through the second bead of the first pair and immediately up through the first bead of the second pair **a**.

2 Pick up one 11º seed bead and pass down through the second bead of the second pair, and immediately up into the first bead of the first pair. Step-up into the first bead added in this row **b**.

There should now be two top beads from which to begin the diamond shape.

3 With the thread exiting out of the first top bead (red), pick up two beads (red, yellow). Pass through the second top bead **c**.

Pick up two beads (yellow, red). Pass through the first top bead (red). Step-up into the first bead added in this row (red). This is the first bead of an edge pair of beads **d**.

4 Pick up two beads (red, yellow). Pass down through the second bead of the edge pair (yellow) **e**.

Work flat peyote for one stitch (blue). The working thread will be exiting a yellow bead **f**.

5 Pick up two beads (yellow, red). Pass down through the second bead of the edge pair (red) **g**. Work flat peyote for one stitch (blue), securing the bead into the red bead added in this round. Step-up into the first bead added in this round (red) **h**.

6 Pick up two beads (red, yellow). Pass down through the second bead of the edge pair of beads **i**.

Work flat peyote for two stitches (blue, blue) **j**.

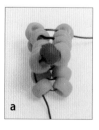

a

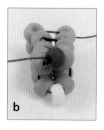

b

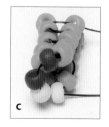

c

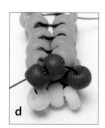

d

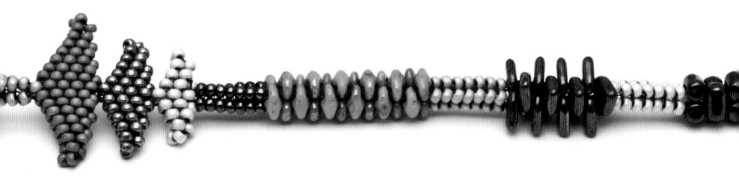

   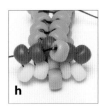  

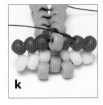  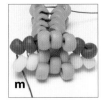   

Pick up two beads (yellow, red). Pass down into the first red bead **k**.

7 Work flat peyote for two stitches (blue, blue). Pass through the two red beads (includes the step-up bead) **l**.

8 Continue in this manner until the desired width is reached. To begin decreasing the diamond shape, don't add new edge beads. Instead, pass directly through the edge bead (red) and directly into the second bead of the edge pair (yellow) **m**.

9 Work three peyote stitches across to the second edge **n**.

10 Exiting the edge bead, turn and pass directly through the second bead of the edge beads without picking up any new edge beads **o**. Work peyote stitch for three stitches **p**.

(directions continue on p. 26)

idea!

Offset the diamond shapes

To add some drama to the harlequin diamond, add one bead on either side of the final two-bead pair and work another harlequin diamond that will be turned 90 degrees from the first one.

To add more drama, use a drop bead instead of the outer edge beads. Both of these ideas can be seen in this bracelet.

BEaDS

11º seed beads
long drops (optional)

q

r

s

t

u

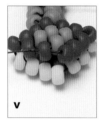

v

w

11 Turn and pass directly through the edge bead and step-up into the first bead of the last round. Work peyote for two stitches **q**. Without picking up any additional beads, connect to the other side as shown.

12 Work peyote across the side **r**.

13 Connect to the other side and step-up into the first bead of this round **s**. Work peyote for one stitch **t**. Connect to the other side **u**. Work peyote for one last stitch **v**. Connect and step-up **w**.

There are now two beads at the top, from which to continue tubular skinny herringbone. Add two beads to each side to create a four-bead base once again. Or, simply play around with this two-bead base to create another harlequin diamond or perhaps something new.

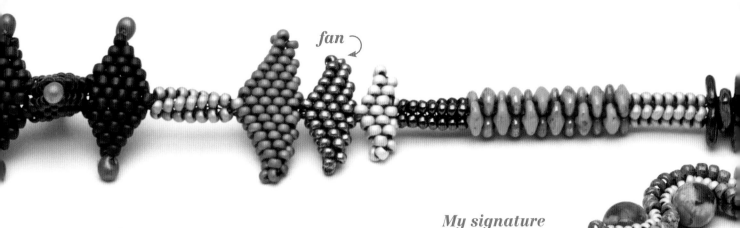

fan

TECHNIQUE
FaN

My signature toggle clasp

I use this Fan Technique as a signature toggle clasp for many of my pieces. Because it's is so near and dear to my heart, I actually debated with myself about whether or not I would share it, but in the end, I know that it will always be my signature toggle, no matter who else may want to use it. The technique as a standalone is simply half of the Harlequin Diamond technique. The half-diamond is then closed using a zigzag method.

1 Here is a stitched half-diamond. I used a different bead color for the last round to make it easier to see the protruding beads, which I will be zigzagging through to close the opening **a–c**.

2 With the thread exiting one of the edge beads, pick up one bead and pass through the second edge bead **d**.

3 Pick up one bead and pass through the protruding bead on the opposite side of the half-diamond **e**.

4 Pick up one bead and pass through the protruding bead on the opposite side of the half-diamond **f**. Continue this zigzag until the end is reached **g**.

5 Add one bead on the edge **h**. Pass through the first "zigzag" bead and then through the protruding bead on the opposite side. Make sure the zigzag bead is straight. If it is not, you may have entered the bead from the wrong side **i**.

6 Pass through the next zigzag bead and then through the protruding bead on the opposite side. Again, make sure the zigzag bead is straight **j**. Continue in this manner all the way across to completely close the half-diamond **k**. Here is another view **l**.

On the rope...

Notice that I have created a string of fan shapes (green, silver, and white). In order to do this, it is necessary to maneuver the thread back to the middle of the existing fan to begin a new fan. If the center bead is a zigzag bead, you'll need to create a new two-bead base. If the center beads are the old protruding beads, just use them to create a new base.

The exaggerated fan that is shown above is created when larger beads are used as the zigzag beads. The larger beads just naturally push the fan out.

a

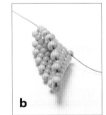

b

c

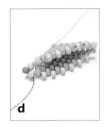

d

e

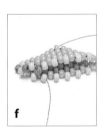

f

g

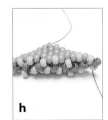

h

i

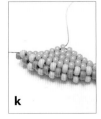

j

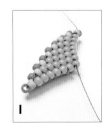

k

l

Try zen garden with...

SuperDuos ↻

two-hole triangles

BeaDS

SuperDuos or any two-hole bead
11º seed beads for skinny
herringbone base

TECHNIQUE
ZEN GARDEN

This technique is one of my very favorites! As soon as two-hole beads (SuperDuos and Twins) hit the market, I created a way to offset them. The end result reminded me of stacked rocks in a peaceful garden, and the name zen garden immediately came to mind. This technique can be done on a three- or four-bead base using any two-hole beads. This sample is created on a four-bead base of tubular skinny herringbone.

1 Pick up one SuperDuo bead. Make a U-turn and pass down through the second hole of the SuperDuo and down into the second bead of the first pair of the skinny herringbone stitch **a**.

2 Pass up through the first bead of the second pair of beads **b**.

3 Pick up one SuperDuo. Make a U-turn and pass down through the second hole of the SuperDuo and down into the second bead of the bead pair **c**.

4 Finish the herringbone stitch, making sure to pass up into the first hole of the first SuperDuo added in this round **d**.
   At this point, the direction of the stitch will change.

5 Pick up one SuperDuo and pass down through the empty hole of the SuperDuo, the first hole of the opposite SuperDuo, and up through the second hole **e**.

6 Pass up through the second hole.

7 Pick up one SuperDuo and pass down through the first hole of the SuperDuo **f** and up through the second hole and the first hole of the first Super-Duo added in this round **g**.
   Change direction again **h**.

8 Pick up one SuperDuo, cross over to the other SuperDuo to secure, and then pass up the second hole.

9 Pick up one SuperDuo, cross over to the other SuperDuo to secure, and pass

Comparing SuperDuos and Twin beads

Twin beads are a seed bead. The glass cane is pulled through a shaping mold and then polished and coated. A SuperDuo is not technically a seed bead. It is a pressed bead mimicking the original Twin bead but with a pinched center. Pressed beads are more expensive, but are more uniform and offer more colors and coatings.
—*Perry Bookstein*

Rulla beads

half Tilas

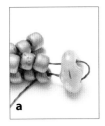 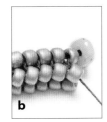 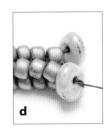 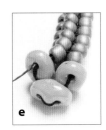 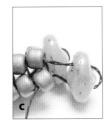

 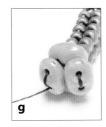 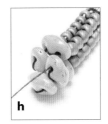 

up through the second hole to finish the stitch. Pass up through the first hole of the first SuperDuo added in this round to set up for the next round **i**.

Continue working in this manner, changing direction every round.

On the rope...

Another bead, another look. When these two-holed triangle beads came to market, I knew they would give this technique an entirely new look.

idea! *Skinny herringbone and zen garden bangle*

To create this bracelet (or make it longer into a necklace), stitch five rows of skinny tubular herringbone and alternate with five rows of zen garden. For this bracelet, I used teal gray 11º seed beads contrasted with silky light gold Twin beads. A project incorporating a three-bead base zen garden can be found on p. 67.

Beads

1.5mm (or 1.8mm) cube beads

11º seed beads

8º seed beads

FLAT TRIANGLE

This skinny tubular herringbone variation uses an increasing technique.

1 Stitch one row of skinny tubular herringbone (two bead pairs) using cube beads **a**.

2 Pick up two cubes. Pass down through the second bead of the first pair. Add one 11º seed bead before connecting to the second pair **b**.

3 Pass up through the first bead of the second pair. Pick up two cubes and pass down through the second bead of the cube pair. Pick up one 11º and pass up into the first bead of the other pair. Finish the round by stepping up into the first bead of the first pair added in this round **c**.

4 Pick up two cubes. Pass down through the second bead of the pair. Add two 11ºs and connect to the second bead pair. Pass up into the first bead of the opposite pair **d**.

5 Pick up two cubes. Add two 11ºs and connect to the other pair. Finish the row and step-up. Repeat, adding three 11ºs between the cube bead stitches. Step-up **e**. Repeat, adding four 11ºs between the cube bead stitches. Step-up **f**.

6 Pick up two 8º seed beads. Pass down into the second bead of the cube pair. Add five 11ºs before connecting to the second pair. Pass up into the first bead of the cube pair **g**.

7 Pick up two 8ºs. Pass down into the second bead of the pair. Add five 11ºs before connecting to the other pair **h**. Weave over to the middle (red beads here) to be in position to continue.

On the rope...
Widen the flat triangle with more rows.

a

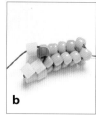

b

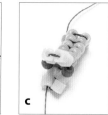

c

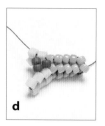

d

e

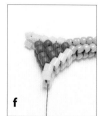

f

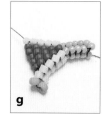

g

h

BeaDs

11º seed beads (colors A and B)

1.8 mm (or 1.5 mm) Japanese cube beads

3.4 mm Japanese drop beads

2 or 3 8mm gemstone beads

Diamond stitch is a straightforward stitch and like many of the stitches I work with, it takes on a different look when beads of different shapes and size are combined. Much like the skinny herringbone wave technique, this diamond stitch variation results from changing the order of the beads used to give it a curve. The larger stones are added during the stitching process.

1 Pick up (**PU**) four cube beads. Create a circle by passing through the first bead in the same direction. The working thread and tail thread should be exiting the same bead in opposite directions **a**.

2 PU one drop bead. Pass through (**PT**) both cube beads to secure **b**.

3 PU one color A 11º seed bead. PT the next two cubes to secure **c**.

4 To position the thread for the next round and step-up (**SU**) by passing through the drop bead **d**.

5 PU two cubes. PT an 11º to secure. Remember to no longer use the base beads **e**.

6 PU two cubes. PT the drop bead to secure. SU into the first cube bead added in this round **f**.

7 PU one color B 11º seed bead. PT two consecutive cubes to secure **g**. DO NOT PT the cube.

8 PU one B 11º. PT two consecutive cubes to secure. Do not PT the drop bead. SU into the next 11º **h**.

9 PU two cubes. PT B 11º to secure **i**.

10 PU two cubes. PT B 11º to secure. SU by passing through the first cube added in this round **j**.

11 PU one A 11º. PT two consecutive cubes.

12 PU one drop bead. PT two consecutive cubes. SU by passing through the next bead **k**.

13 PU two cubes. PT the drop bead to secure.

14 PU two cubes. PT the A 11º to secure. SU by passing through the first cube added in this round.

15 PU one B 11º. PT two consecutive cubes to secure.

16 PU one B 11°. PT two consecutive cubes to secure. SU by passing through the next bead.

17 PU two cubes. PT the B 11º to secure.

18 PU two cubes. PT the B 11º to secure. SU through the first cube added in this round.

19 Repeat steps 2–18.

20 Repeat steps 2–5.

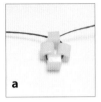

a

b

c

d

e

f

g

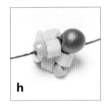

h

i

j

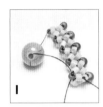

k

l

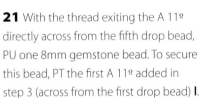

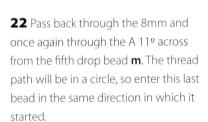

m

n

o

p

q

ADD THE FIRST ACCENT BEAD

Read through the instructions to get a good mental picture of what to do.

21 With the thread exiting the A 11º directly across from the fifth drop bead, PU one 8mm gemstone bead. To secure this bead, PT the first A 11º added in step 3 (across from the first drop bead) **l**.

22 Pass back through the 8mm and once again through the A 11º across from the fifth drop bead **m**. The thread path will be in a circle, so enter this last bead in the same direction in which it started.

NOTE: The beaded rope wraps snug to the 8mm gemstone so that none of the thread shows **n.**

The thread should now be in position to add the second set of cubes (see step 6) to complete the row started before adding the 8mm gemstone. If not, check to see that the A 11º was added in the correct direction.

Remember, there are only three types of rows being stitched. One adds two sets of cubes, one adds two B 11ºs, and one adds one drop and one A 11º.

To continue, follow these shortened instructions:

NOTE: The drop bead should be on the opposite side so that these new drop beads wrap around the 8mm gemstone added in step 24. Refer to **o.**

23 Counting from left to right, add the sixth drop bead. Continue until there are a total of 10 drop bead **p**.

ADD THE NEXT ACCENT BEAD

24 Add the next 8mm gemstone bead in the same manner as the first one. Continue working until three more drop beads have been added. Make sure these are on the side opposite the last five. Finish the rope with an B 11º row **q**.

BAIL

Follow these instructions row by row:

25 Add two A 11ºs between each of the two B 11ºs.

26 Add one A 11º between each of the four A 11ºs.

27 Add two A 11ºs between each of the four A 11ºs.

28 Add one A 11º between each of the eight A 11ºs.

29 Add one cube bead between each of the eight A 11ºs.

30 Add one drop bead between each of the eight cubes. To complete the bail, make sure the thread is exiting from the drop bead that is in the same line as the B 11º.

31 PU three cubes and PT the opposite drop bead. PU three cubes and PT the drop bead from the start. Circle the thread around all of these beads twice to strengthen and secure.

Weave the thread through the beads, tying knots along the way. Weave in the tail thread.

TECHNIQUE
DIAMOND STITCH BALL VARIATION

This is stitched on a four-bead base using 6º seed beads, 8º seed beads, 11º seed beads, and 10º triangle beads. The different size beads create the ball shape. Don't forget to step-up at the end of each round.

1 On a four-bead base (or to begin), start with a round of 11º seed beads. The working thread is on the left **a**.

2 Add one 10º triangle bead between each 11º. Step-up. The working thread is on the left **b**.

3 Add two 8º seed beads between each triangle. Step-up into the first bead of the first pair of beads added in this round. The working thread is on the left **c**.

4 Add one 6º seed bead **within** each pair of 8ºs. Step-up **d**. Guess which side the working thread is on? Left, of course!

5 Add two 8ºs between each 6º. Step-up. Gently pull these beads into a cup shape. The working thread is on the left **e**.

6 Add one triangle within each pair of 8ºs. Step-up. The working thread is on the left **f**.

7 Add one 11º between each triangle. Step-up. The working thread is on the left **g**.

a

b

c

d

e

f

g

TECHNIQUE
BASKET WEAVE ON A FOUR-BEAD BASE

These instructions are written row by row, continuing on a four-bead base. If this is the beginning of a new project, simply begin with a four-bead base of 11º seed beads and skip to step 2.

Use 11º seed beads and 1.5mm (or 1.8mm) cube beads.

1 Add one 11º seed bead between each of the four beads from the base. Step-up **a**.

2 Add one 11º between **each** 11º, for a total of four beads added in this round. Step-up **b**.

3 Add two cubes between **each** 11º, for a total of eight beads added in this round. Step-up **c**.

4 Add one 11º between **each** cube, for a total of eight beads added in this round. Step-up **d**.

5 Add two 11ºs between **each** 11º as you begin the diamond stitch, for a total of 16 beads added in this round. Step-up **e**.

6 Continue adding beads as follows:

• One cube within each 11º pair (eight beads); remember that after adding the cubes, you will pass through the second bead of the pair and directly up into the first bead of the next pair. Step-up. **f**

• Two 11ºs between each cube (16 beads). Step-up into the first bead of the first pair added in this round. Gently pull the beads into a cup shape **g**.

• One 11º within each 11º pair (eight beads). Step-up **h**.

• Two 11ºs between each 11º (16 beads). Step-up **i**.

• One cube within each 11º pair (eight beads). Step-up **j**.

• Two 11ºs between each cube bead (16 beads). Step-up **k**.

• One 11º within each 11º pair (eight beads). Step-up **l**.

7 Add one cube between each 11º (eight beads). Step-up **m**.

8 Add one 11º and pass through the next two cubes. Repeat three more times (four beads). Step-up **n**.

9 Add one 11º between each bead (four beads). Step-up **o**.

10 Add one bead between each bead (four beads). Step-up **p**. This bead can be different, as in the start of a new section.

Repeat the center section as desired to shorten or elongate the basket.

Bead tip!

When you are nearing the end of the thread and the thread keeps pulling out of the needle, tie a knot at the very end of the tail thread. Now the thread can't pull out!

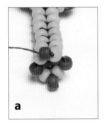
a

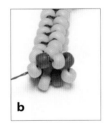
b

c

d

e

f

g

h

i

j

k

l

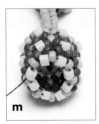
m

n

o

p

15º seed bead

11º seed bead

8º seed bead

10º Delica

11º seed bead

8º sharp triangle

*two-hole triangle

6º seed bead

11º seed bead

11º seed bead

8º rounded triangle

11º seed bead

O-bead

8º Delica

long magatama

8º hex

11º sharp triangle

11º seed beads

11º seed bead

8º one-cut

11º seed bead

11º seed bead

Rizo

11º seed bead

6º rounded triangle

6º baroque finish

long drop

8º seed bead

3mm cube

11º seed bead

Super Duo*

3mm cube

10º round triangle

8º seed bead

8º seed bead

SuperUno

8º seed bead

1.5mm cube

11º seed bead

8º seed bead

12º three-cut

11º hex

8º seed bead

11º seed bead

TECHNIQUE
TUBULAR PEYOTE USING A FOUR-BEAD BASE

This technique was included in *Seed Bead Stitching* and the three-bead technique is illustrated on p. 8. Work the stitch the same way using four beads instead of three. This long section uses many of the same beads as the skinny tubular herringbone section. I love the way the beads undulate along the rope.

spiral tubular peyote   *peyote bumps*

TECHNIQUE
SPIRAL TUBULAR PEYOTE

Spiral tubular peyote is a playful variation of tubular peyote. Each bead in the round is different.

Using a four-bead base, add one 11º seed bead for the first stitch, a 1.5mm or 1.8mm cube bead for the next stitch, an 8º triangle bead for the next stitch, and a 3.4mm drop bead for the last stitch. Step-up into the 11º to position for the next round **a**.

Add one bead for each stitch in the same order as above: one 11º, one 1.5mm or 1.8mm cube, one 8º triangle, and one 3.4mm drop. Step-up into the 11ºs. Notice that the bead added for each stitch is the same bead the thread is exiting. Repeat this pattern until the desired length is reached **b–d**.

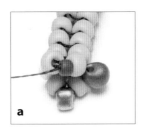
a

b

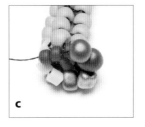
c

d

TECHNIQUE
PEYOTE BUMPS

Playtime! I just showed what the rope will look like when a different bead is added for each stitch in a round, but what will happen when a different bead is added for each round? Well, when different beads are added in graduated sizes (up and down), this cute little "bump" appears. Create the bump shown here using beads in the following order: 11º seed bead, cube, 8º seed bead, 6º seed bead **e**.

To help these bumps stand apart from each other, create a short section between each bump using either tubular peyote or tubular skinny herringbone in 11ºs or 15ºs.

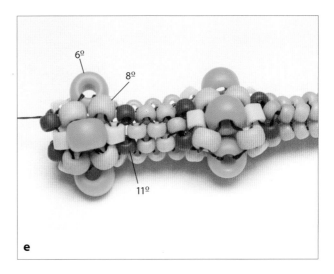
e

37

TECHNIQUE
PEYOTE BALL

As shown on the rope, beads of different shapes and sizes create "balls" that look very different. Three rows of tubular peyote separate each ball, which are made on a four-bead base. Peyote balls on a three-bead base are shown on p. 48.

The photos here show 8º seed beads in two different colors (A and B). The balls on the main rope are created using 8º seed beads, 6º seed beads, 11º seed beads, O-beads, triangle beads, and cube beads.

1 Begin with a four-bead base of 11º seed beads. For illustration purposes, 8º seed beads in two colors (A and B) will be used for all of the steps. Add one color A 8º between each of the four 11º base beads (four beads total) **a**. Step-up.

2 Add two B 8ºs between each of the A 8ºs (eight beads total) **b**. Step-up.

3 Add one A 8º between each B 8º (eight beads total) **c**. Step-up.

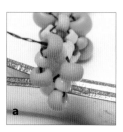

a

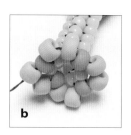

b

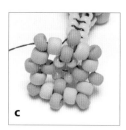

c

 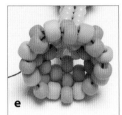 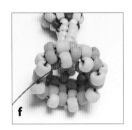  

4 Add one B 8º between each A 8º (eight beads total) **d**. Step-up.

5 Add one A 8º between each B 8º (eight beads total) **e**. Step-up.

6 Add one B 8º between each A 8º (eight beads total) **f**. Step-up.

7 Without picking up a bead, pass through the next protruding bead. Pick up one A and pass through the next two protruding Bs. Repeat two more times. Pick up one bead and pass

through the next two protruding beads (the second of which is the first bead you passed through at the start of this step). Step-up. There will be a total of four As added in this round **g**.

8 Add one 11º between each A 8º **h**. This will be the base for the next section.

8º hex

10º delica

11º seed bead

10º delica

8º seed bead

8º triangle

6º seed bead

saucers

TECHNIQUE
PEYOTE SAUCER

I suggest using two colors of 11º seed beads (A and B) while learning this variation.

1 Using a four-bead base, add one A 11º between each base bead **a**. Step-up.

2 Add two B 11ºs between each A 11º bead for a total of eight beads **b**. Step-up.

3 Add one A 11º between each B 11º bead for a total of eight beads **c**. Step-up.

4 Add two B 11ºs between each A 11º for a total of 16 beads **d**. Step-up.

5 Add one A 11º within each B 11º pair for a total of eight beads **e**. Step-up.

6 Add two B 11ºs between each A 11º for a total of 16 beads **f**. Step-up.

7 Add one A 11º within each B 11º pair for a total of eight beads **g**. Step-up.

8 Add one B 11º between each A 11º for a total of eight beads **h**. Step-up.

9 Without picking up a bead, pass through the next protruding B 11º. Pick up one A 11º. Pass through the next two B 11º protruding beads. Pick up one A 11º. Pass through the next two protruding B 11ºs. Pick up one A 11º and pass through the next two protruding B 11ºs (these are the two beads you passed through at the beginning of this round) **i**. Step-up.

10 Add one bead between each A 11º added in the previous round. This bead will be the first bead of the next section or transition section.

On the rope...

Peyote saucers from left to right use: 11º seed beads (gold); 8º seed beads (red); cube and drop bead combination (gray); 10º triangle (burgundy); 6º seed beads (olive).

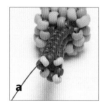

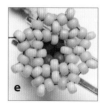

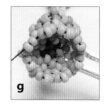
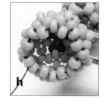

ruffled disk

TECHNIQUE
PEYOTE RUFFLED DISK

These disks can be made with any type of bead on a three- or four-bead base. Some beads will create a more obvious ruffle/wave than others. I like to work a few rows of a tubular stitch between ruffles to keep them separated. For this ruffle, I have chosen to use 8º beads in two colors (A and B) on an 11º bead base to make each round easier to see.

1 On an 11º seed bead base, add one color A 8º seed bead between each base bead for a total of four new beads. Step-up **a**.

2 Add two color B 8º seed beads between each A 8º for a total of eight new beads **b**. Step-up.

3 Add one A 8º between each B 8º for a total of eight new beads **c**. Step-up.

Stop here or continue another round.

4 Add two B 8ºs between each A 8º for a total of 16 beads **d**. Step-up.

Stop here or continue another round.

5 Add one A 8º between each B 8º for a total of 16 beads **e**. Step-up.

The disk will be wavy **f**.

6 Carefully weave the thread back through the beads until the thread is exiting one of the four center beads.

a

b

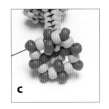

c

d

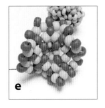

e

f

folded peyote ruffle

peyote puffy squares

TECHNIQUE
FOLDED PEYOTE RUFFLE

This peyote ruffle variation adds texture to the rope and is simply fun to do. Create a peyote ruffled disk (p. 41) any size as long it ends on a single bead round. With the thread exiting one of the outer single beads as shown **a**, pick up two 11º seed beads and pass through the single bead on the opposite side **b**.

Pick up two 11ºs, and pass through the bead that the thread was exiting in the last step, and step-up into the first 11º added in the last step **c**.

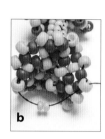

TECHNIQUE
PEYOTE PUFFY SQUARE

1 Add one 11º seed bead between each of the four base beads **a**. Step-up.

2 Add two 11ºs between each of the 11ºs. Step-up into the first bead of the first pair of beads added in this round **b**.

3 With the thread exiting the first bead of the pair, pick up two 11ºs and pass down through the second bead of the pair **c**.

4 Notice the space before the next pair of beads. Fill in this space with one 11º and secure by passing up into the first bead of the next pair **d**.

5 Pick up two 11ºs and pass down through the second bead of this bead pair.

6 Using one 11º, fill in the space before the next pair and secure by passing up into the first bead of the pair.

7 Repeat steps 5 and 6 twice.

8 Step-up by passing into the first bead of the first pair added in this round **e**. Look at the structure of this shape. Each pair of beads is sitting at a corner and will be worked in herringbone fashion. The beads along each side are worked in peyote stitch and increase by one for each round. The sample here is worked in five rounds. The samples on the rope are created with four rounds.

Close the shape by decreasing as follows:

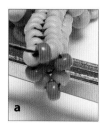

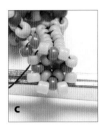  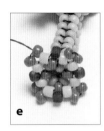  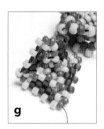 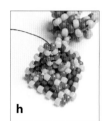

9 With the thread exiting the first bead of a bead pair, pass directly into the second bead of the pair without picking up any additional beads **f**.

10 Work peyote to the next corner.

11 With the thread exiting the first bead of the corner pair, pass directly down into the second bead without picking up any additional beads.

12 Work peyote to the next corner **g**. Repeat steps 11 and 12 twice **h**.

13 To step-up, pass down through the second bead of the corner pair and into the first bead on the peyote stitch side **i**.

14 Work peyote for three stitches **j**.

15 DO NOT pass through the two corner beads. Pass directly into the first peyote stitch on the next side. The thread will not show when the shape begins to tighten **k**.

16 Work peyote for three stitches.

17 Skip over the two corner beads and pass into the first peyote stitch on the next side.

18 Repeat steps 16 and 17. Repeat step 16.

19 Skip over the two corner beads. Pass into the first peyote stitch AND the first peyote stitch from this round **l**.

20 Work peyote for two stitches **m**.

21 Pass directly into the first peyote stitch on the next side (orange) **n**.

22 Repeat steps 20 and 21 twice.

23 Repeat steps 20 and 21, making sure to step-up by passing into the first peyote stitch in this new round **o**.

24 Work one peyote stitch.

25 Pass directly into the first peyote stitch (blue) on the next side.

26 Repeat steps 24 and 25 three times.

27 Step-up into the first peyote stitch of this round **p**.

28 Add one 11º between each of the four beads from the last round. These four beads are the base for the next section.

On the rope...
Create peyote puffy squares using 11º, 8º, and 15º seed beads.

accent bead 4 to 3

seamless 4 to 3

accent bead 3 to 4

TECHNIQUE
TRANSITIONS

I have developed two different ways to move from techniques requiring a three-bead base to techniques requiring a four-bead base and vice versa. The first transition is to add an accent bead to separate the sections. Adding this bead so that it stays centered is the important part. The second way uses seed beads for a seamless transition.

ACCENT BEAD TRANSITIONS

FOUR-BEAD TO THREE-BEAD

Follow the diagram below. With the thread exiting bead 1, pick up an accent bead. Pick up bead 2. Pass back through the AB. Pass through beads 3 and 4. Pass back through the AB. Pick up bead 5. Pass back through the AB. Pass through bead 6. Pass back through the AB. Pick up bead 7. Pass back through the AB. Pass through bead 1. Pass back through the AB and any one of the beads on the three-bead side **a**. Continue with a three-bead base technique.

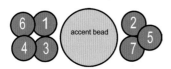

On the rope, I have stitched a few rows of three-bead tubular peyote (instructions, p. 8), to create a little space before transitioning back to the a four-bead base.

THREE-BEAD TO FOUR-BEAD

Follow the diagram below. With the thread exiting bead 1, pick up an accent bead (AB). Pick up beads 2 and 3. Pass through the AB. Pass through bead 4. Pass through the AB. Pick up beads 5 and 6. Pass through the AB. Pass through bead 7. Pass through the AB and any one of the beads on the new four-bead side. Continue with a four-bead base technique **b**.

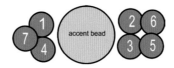

On the main rope I have stitched a few rows of skinny tubular herringbone to create a little space before seamlessly transitioning back to a three-bead base (beginning with step 7 as described).

SEAMLESS TRANSITIONS WITH SEED BEADS

Beadwork is very mathematical for me. The reward of figuring it all out far outweighs the frustrations along the way, and this technique is no exception. Using my knowledge of common denominators, I know that I need 12 beads in the middle of the transition. This technique is NOT perfectly symmetrical, but it gets the job done.

To transition from a three-bead base to a four-bead base, begin at Step 1. To transition from a four-bead base to a three-bead base, begin at Step 7.

TRANSITION FROM A THREE-BEAD TO A FOUR-BEAD BASE

1 Begin with a three-bead base.

2 Add two beads (blue) between each of the three beads.

3 Add one bead (green) between each of the six beads.

4 Add two beads (yellow) between each of the six beads.

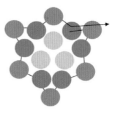

5 Add one bead (blue) between each of the 12 beads.

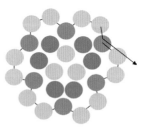

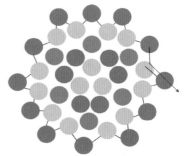

6 With the thread exiting the first bead added in the last step, pick up two beads (green). Skip over five edge beads and pass through the sixth bead, which is directly across from the starting bead. Pick up two beads (green). Skip over five edge beads and pass through the beginning bead. The green beads are the new four-bead base.

NOTE: These six beads will be pulled tight, which will force the beads to curl up. Unused beads are gray.

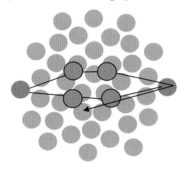

TRANSITION FROM A FOUR-BEAD TO A THREE-BEAD BASE

NOTE: In steps 7–9, the gray beads have been eliminated in order to make it easier to see the bead placements.

7 With the thread exiting between the first pair of beads added in the previous step, pick up one bead. Pass through the second bead of the pair. Pick up two beads. Pass through the first bead of the second pair. Pick up one bead. Pass through the second bead of the pair. Pick up the last two beads. Pass through the first bead of the first (green) pair. Step-up into the first bead added in this round.

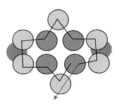

8 Add two beads (blue) between each of the beads added in the previous step for a total of 12 beads added.

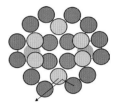

9 Add one bead (green) between each bead added in the previous step.

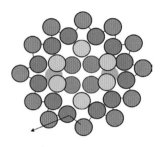

10 Add three beads (blue) between every fourth bead from the previous round (unused beads are gray). Pass the needle back through the first two beads added in this round. The thread will be exiting from a center bead.

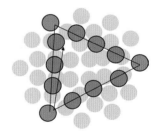

11 Circle through each of the center beads to create the new three-bead base. Be sure to gently pull these three beads together.

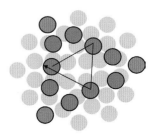

An AHA! moment

As my work continued to evolve and as I continued to play, I realized that I could do another four-to-three transition by taking the "four" down to a "two" and adding three beads between each of the new two base beads. This gives a six-bead base from which a three-bead base can be created by adding one bead between every two beads. Tah-dah!

To reverse this from a three-bead base back to a four-bead base, add two beads between each of the three base beads for a total of six beads, and then add one bead between each group of three beads, which creates a new two-bead base, which can then be turned into a four-bead base. A lot of words for a simple process. I will use this technique to transition from a three-bead base to a four-bead when I complete the three-bead section.

TECHNIQUE
TUBULAR PEYOTE VARIATIONS

The following techniques illustrate a variety of stitches and stitch variations using a three-bead base.

A rope of three-bead peyote stitch won't really look much different than the four-bead rope shown on p. 36.

PEYOTE BUMPS

This technique was detailed on p. 37 using a four-bead base. See more of this technique with Berries for Breakfast (p. 84). For this sample I have selected graduating sizes (11º, 8º, and 6º) of one color family. The first bump uses each bead for one round. The second bump uses each bead for two rounds, and the last bump uses each bead for three rounds. I love to play!

PEYOTE SPIRAL

This technique is shown on p. 37 using a four-bead base. Skip step 1 if the spiral is going to be on an already established three-bead base.

1 Pick up three 11º seed beads and create a circle by passing back through the first bead in the round. The working thread and tail thread will be exiting from the same bead (1) in opposite directions.

With the thread exiting the first 11º (1), pick up one cube bead (4) and pass through the second

11º (2). Pick up one triangle bead (5) and pass through the third 11º (3). Pick up one drop bead (6) and pass though the first 11º (1).

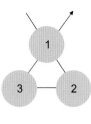

2 Pass through the cube bead (4) to step-up.

NOTE: The beads will pull into a tube and will not lie flat as shown in the drawings.

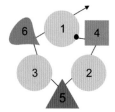

3 With the thread exiting bead 4, pick up one cube and pass though bead 5. Pick up one triangle bead (8) and pass through bead 6. Pick up one drop bead (9) and pass through bead 4. Step-up into the first cube (7) to begin the next round.

4 Work in this manner for any number of rows. Be sure to step-up at the end of each round.

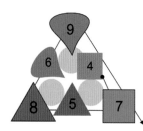

peyote spiral

peyote saucer

a

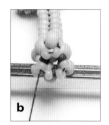
b

c

d

e

f

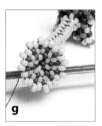
g

h

i

j

k

On the rope...

This peyote spiral uses 1.8mm cube beads, 8º rounded triangle beads, and Rizo beads.

PEYOTE SAUCER 2

This tubular peyote variation (three-bead base) was so much fun to watch form. I like the look of the smaller beads as the base. I used one color each of 15º seed beads and 11º seed beads. At this point, written instructions should be easy to follow and understand.

1 Add one 15º seed bead between each of the three beads from the three-bead base for a total of three new beads **a**. Step-up.

2 Add two 15ºs between each of the three beads for a total of six new beads **b**. Step-up.

3 Add one 15º between each of the six beads for a total of six new beads **c**. Step-up.

4 Add two 15ºs between each of the six beads for a total of 12 new beads **d**. Step-up.

5 Add one 15º between each of the 12 beads for a total of 12 new beads **e**. Step-up.

6 Add one 11º seed bead between each of the 12 15ºs **f**. Step-up.

7 Add one 11º between each of the 12 11ºs **g**. Step-up.

8 Add one 11º between each of the 12 11ºs **h**. Step-up. Note that the shape will begin to cup.

9 Add one 15º between each of the 12 11ºs **i**. Step-up.

10 Add one 15º between each of the 12 15ºs **j**. Step-up.

11 Pick up one 15º and pass through the next two beads. Repeat until the round is complete. Six beads will have been used in this round.

12 Add one 15º between each of the six 15ºs. Step-up.

13 Pick up one 15º. Pass through the next two beads and add one 15º. Repeat **k**. Three beads will have been used in this round.

14 Pass through the three beads again to tighten, if desired, or just continue working.

On the rope...

The larger saucer uses 11º and 8º seed beads. It is a little tricky to stitch, because the beads start to wave and need some loving coaxing to get into place.

PEYOTE BALLS

There are many variations of this technique, which can be created from either a three-bead base or a four-bead base, the latter of which was shown on p. 38. The following instructions and illustrations are for a three-bead base.

1 Add one bead between each of the three base beads.

2 Add two beads between each of the beads from step 2 for a total of six beads. Step-up.

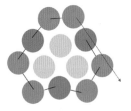

3 Add one bead between each of the six beads. Step-up.

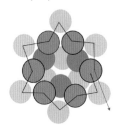

4 Start pulling the beads inward. Add one bead between each of the six beads. Step-up.

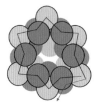

5 Without picking up a bead, pass through the next bead (blue). Pick up one bead (green) and pass through the next two beads. Pick up one bead (green) and pass through the next two beads (blue). Pick up one bead (green) and pass through the next two beads (blue). Pass up into the first bead added (green) to finish (7).

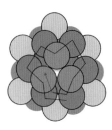

Pass through the last three beads again to tighten. Continue with a transition stitch and another peyote ball or other technique. On the rope, I have created peyote balls using several different beads, beginning with 8º seed beads. Next balls are as follows: 11º seed beads, 6º seed beads, Rizo beads, O-beads, and 15º seed beads.

Here are the instructions for another, bigger, peyote ball.

Begin with a three-bead base.

Add one bead between each bead (three beads).

Add two beads between each bead (six beads).

Add one bead between each bead (six beads).

Add two beads between each bead (12 beads).

Add one bead within each pair of beads added in the previous round (six beads).

Add two beads between each bead (12 beads).

Add one bead within each pair of beads added in the previous round (six beads).

Add one bead between each bead (six beads).

Without picking up a bead, pass through the next bead.

Add one bead and pass through two beads.

Add one bead and pass through two beads.

Add one bead and pass through two beads.

Step-up into the first bead added in this round.

Circle back through the three beads to tighten.

play!

On the rope...

Combine 11º seed beads with Rizo beads for this cool starburst effect (red beads)! From right to left, here are the beads used for the rest of the balls: 6º seed beads, 11º seed beads, O-beads, Rizo beads, 6º seed beads, 11º seed beads, and 8º seed beads.

Although these "peyote" balls are actually a combination of peyote and diamond stitch, I chose to put them here to go along with the peyote balls.

technique
BOBBE STITCH

A story...I like to imagine that just like me, many beaders are looking for a new way to manipulate beads that is not only really cool, but that others grab onto and enjoy using in their work.

While playing with tubular herringbone, I wondered what would happen if, after I picked up two beads, I didn't pass my needle "down" into the second bead of a pair, but instead passed it directly "up" into the first bead of the next pair. I tried it for one round and noticed that the beads I did not pass into just naturally stuck out. I repeated this for another round, and of course, the beads I did not pass through also stuck out. For the third round, I used just one bead per stitch, I loved the way this looked and loved the ideas that were rushing through my head. Using the three beads as a new "base," I repeated the pattern. For lack of another name, I called this stitch "122." Not very creative, but it allowed me to remember how to create the stitch. And of course, I had to design a project, so I stitched a bracelet using beads on my bead board (p. 53).

Shortly after creating the bracelet, I was teaching the stitch (and bracelet) to a small group of beaders, and without even thinking about it, I called the bracelet the "Bobbe Bracelet" and then decided then and there to name the technique the Bobbe Stitch after a dear friend. Over the past few years since I created this technique, I have varied it, expanded on it, and challenged myself to find new ways to use it. It is one of my favorite stitches.

These are the instructions for the original "122," now named the Bobbe Stitch.

I strongly suggest using a different color bead for each round while learning this stitch. It is very easy to get lost because the beads do not line up neatly. The stitch has a slight twist and a bit of an organic look. The fun of this stitch comes with experimenting with different bead combinations.

THE "1" ROUND

1 Begin with a base of three beads (1, 2, and 3). If this is the beginning of a new project, create a circle by passing through the first bead strung in the direction strung. The working thread and tail thread should be exiting from the same bead in opposite directions. If working off an existing three-bead base, simply add one bead between each of the three beads in the base **a**.

THE FIRST "2" ROUND

2 Pick up two beads (4 and 5) and pass through bead 2.

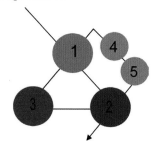

3 Pick up two beads (6 and 7) and pass through bead 3.

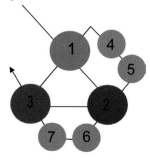

4 Pick up two beads (8 and 9) and pass through bead 1.

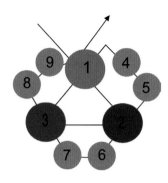

5 To get ready for the next round, step-up by passing the needle through bead 4 (the first bead added in this round) **b**.

NOTE: For the next and subsequent rounds, all previous rows shown in the illustrations are grayed and the numbers have been eliminated to make the drawings clean and readable.

Please notice in the illustration that beads 4 and 5 are a pair, beads 6 and 7 are a pair, and beads 8 and 9 are a pair.

THE SECOND "2" ROUND

6 With the needle exiting bead 4 (the first bead of the first pair of beads), pick up two beads (10 and 11). Skip over bead 5 (the second bead of the first pair) and pass the needle directly up

into bead 6 (the first bead of the next pair) **c**.

7 With the needle exiting up from bead 6 (the first bead of the second pair of beads), pick up two beads (12 and 13). Skip over bead 7 (the second bead of the second pair) and pass the needle up directly into bead 8, which is the first bead of the next pair **d**.

8 With the needle exiting up from bead 8 (the first bead of the third pair of beads), pick up two beads (14 and 15). Skip over bead 9 (the second bead of the third pair) and pass the needle up directly into bead 4 (the first bead of the previous round).

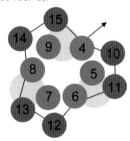

9 To get ready for the next round, step-up by passing directly through bead 10.

This is the first bead of this round just completed **e**.

NOTE: For the beads NOT passed through (beads 5, 7, and 9 in the illustration), make sure that the thread stays on the inside of these beads. If the thread wraps around to the outside, the beads will drop into the center of the tube. This is especially true for drop-style beads. Yes, I know that the illustration looks as though the thread is on the outside of these beads (5, 7, and 9), but that was the best way to do the drawing. Remember that all of the beads added in round 3 actually sit on top of the beads from round 2; they are not actually off to the sides.

To continue on to the next "1" round…

The next round uses one bead per stitch.

Notice that beads 10 and 11 are a pair, beads 12 and 13 are a pair, and beads 14 and 15 are a pair.

a

b

c

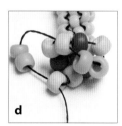
d

e

On the rope...

The beads used on the rope are: 11º round (teal), 8º round (gold), and 6º triangle (brown).

For the next section (red), I wanted to use the fabulous O-beads, but wow, was that confusing using just one color, so I opted for using 8º seed beads along with the O-beads. The "1" round uses one 8º seed bead per stitch, the first "2" round uses two O-beads per stitch, and the second "2" round uses one 8º seed bead and one O-bead.

Make a whole bead-soup bracelet as shown in the next project! A number of variations and Bobbe-inspired techniques will be shown further along on the rope.

10 With the thread exiting up from bead 10 (the first bead of the first pair of beads), pick up one bead (16). Skip over bead 11 (the second bead of the first pair) and pass the needle up through bead 12, which is the first bead of the next pair **f**.

NOTE: As in the previous Note, the thread will not be wrapping bead 11. Keep the thread to the inside, especially if bead 11 is a drop bead.

11 With the thread exiting bead 12 (the first bead of the second pair of beads), pick up one bead (17). Skip over bead 13 (the second bead of the second pair) and pass the needle up through bead 14 (the first bead of the next pair). Keep the thread to the inside.

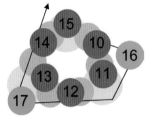

12 With the thread exiting bead 14 (the first bead of the third pair of beads), pick up one bead (18). Skip over bead 15 (the second bead of the third pair) and pass the needle up into bead 10 (the first bead of the first pair of beads added in the previous round). Keep the thread to the inside.

13 To get ready for the next round, step-up by passing the needle through bead 16. This is the first bead of the round just added **g**. Pull these beads tightly into a tube.

The next round uses two beads per stitch, and the following round uses two beads per stitch. The pattern repeats these three steps.

Beads

11º seed beads

1.5 or 1.8 cube beads

top-drilled pearls

Bobbe bracelet

Repeat the instructions (beginning on p. 50) from steps 2–13 until the desired length has been reached.

Finish as desired. If a seamless finish is planned for a bangle bracelet, don't end the length of rope with steps 11–13. Use the original base row of three beads as the ending/connecting three beads.

NOTE: Over time, this stitch has transformed. I don't always use the "122" pattern; I simply use the "2." In other words, I don't have a round of single beads. Each stitch in each round uses two beads, never passing through the second bead of the pair.

Bobbe silver and pearl necklace

To create a necklace similar to this one, follow these easy instructions that repeat every three rounds:

Round 1: three 11º seed beads.

Round 2: two 1.5mm (or 1.8mm) cube beads between each 11º.

Round 3: for the first stitch, add one 11º and one top-drilled pearl. For the second and third stitches of this round, use one 11º and one 1.5mm (or 1.8mm) cube for each pair. Just make sure to never go through the second bead in any bead pair.

I have two great projects which showcase the Bobbe Stitch along with skinny herringbone, but because they require a four-bead base, I have moved them to p. 80 and 82.

TECHNIQUE
PUFFY TRIANGLE

This is one of my favorite techniques. These triangle shapes are a combination of "flat" herringbone stitch and "flat" peyote stitch. Each corner is worked in herringbone and each side is worked in peyote. I like the way different beads create triangles with different looks. You need a three-bead base for this stitch. I recommend using three different colors of 11º seed beads (A, B, and C) while you are learning this technique. Alternate the colors for each row.

This technique is a sister technique to the puffy square (p. 42), using a three-bead base instead of a four-bead base.

1 Choose one of the 11º beads for the base. If this is the first section on the piece, create a circle of beads by passing through the first bead in the direction strung. If this is being added to an existing section, add one bead in between each of the three beads in the previous row to create a new "base" for the technique.

2 Add two beads between each base bead as shown. Be sure to step-up.

3 Add two beads at each corner and one bead along each side. Step-up.

4 Add two beads at each corner and two beads along each side. Step-up.

NOTE: In step 5, the three-dimensional shape will begin to form. The thread should be exiting the first bead of a corner pair. Do not pick up any beads at the three corners.

5 Pass through the second bead of the corner pair. Work three peyote stitches, securing the third stitch into the first bead of the next corner pair. Pass directly through the second corner bead. Repeat entire sequence on the other two sides. Step-up into the first bead of the first peyote stitch.

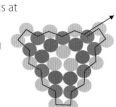

NOTE: At this point, the blue beads need to be bent toward the center of the triangle, on top of the beads already stitched, as the shape begins to close.

6 The blue beads in this illustration are the beads stitched in the last step. The thread is exiting the first blue bead. Stitch two green beads. Follow the thread path, as shown, to begin the next side. Repeat on the third side. Step-up by passing through the first green bead added in this step.

7 Add one bead between each bead pair, as shown, to finish the puffy triangle.

8 Pass through the three center beads one more time to tighten the triangle.

On the rope...

The first three puffy triangles use 8º beads.

Nobody is perfect.....I made this bracelet using one puffy triangle right after another, and for some reason, it broke. I'm guessing there was just too much tension on the beads, but in any case, here is the sample to highlight how different beads look using this technique. The second sample highlights 15º Delica beads separated by mini peyote balls.

PUFFY TRIANGLE & PEYOTE BALLS BRACELET

To create this unique bracelet, stitch puffy triangles (p. 54) separated with peyote balls (p. 38).

On the rope...

Experiment with different beads, as in the next three (brown, blue, and gold).

PUFFY TRIANGLE VARIATION

Instead of using just one bead, try three different beads! This sample uses 11º triangle beads, 6º seed beads, and 8º seed beads.

Beginning with a three-bead base, add one 11º triangle, one 6º, and one 8º (one bead per stitch) for the next round **a**.

Pick up one triangle and one 6º. Secure by passing through the 6º **b**.

Pick up one 6º and one 8º. Secure by passing through the 8º.

Pick up one 8º and one triangle. Secure by passing through the triangle. Step-up into the first bead added in this round (the triangle) **c**.

Pick up one triangle and one 6º. Pass down into the 6º to secure **d**. Work one peyote stitch along the side using a 6º **e**. Pick up one 6º and one 8º. Pass down into the 8º **f**. Work one peyote stitch along the side using an 8º **g**. Pick up one 8º and one triangle. Pass down into the triangle **h**. Work one peyote stitch along the side using a triangle. Step-up into the first bead added in this round (the triangle) **i**. Add corner beads as described above and stitch across each side using peyote stitch **j**. The number of beads across the sides will increase by one for each round stitched. This sample uses two additional rounds.

To close the triangle:

With the thread exiting from the corner triangle, pass directly through the 6º without picking up any additional beads **k**.

a

b

c

d

e

f

Work four peyote stitches to the end using the 6ºs **l**.

Without picking up any additional beads, pass directly into the 8º corner bead **m**.

Work four peyote stitches to the end using the 8ºs.

Without picking up any additional beads, pass directly into the triangle.

Work four peyote stitches to the end using the triangles. Step-up by passing through the corner 6º bead and the first 6º added in this round **n**.

Work peyote for three stitches using the 6ºs. To begin the next side, pass directly into the first protruding 8º. The thread will not show when the triangle is tightened **o**.

Work three peyote stitches using the 8ºs. To begin the next side, pass directly into the first protruding triangle **p**.

Work three peyote stitches using the triangles. To begin the next round, step-up into the first 6º on the side and the first 6º added in this round **q**.

Continue in this manner until the triangle is closed with three beads at the center (one triangle, one 6º, and one 8º). Circle back through these three beads to tighten **r**.

play!

Mixed variation

Here's another triangle using 1.5mm cubes, triangles, and seed beads.

g

h

i

j

k

l

m

n

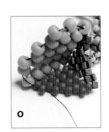

o

p

q

r

pagoda triangle ↶   *diamond stitch variations* ↷

TECHNIQUE
PAGODA TRIANGLE

This puffy triangle variation uses two different shaped and sized beads, which force the curve. I used one color of 10º triangle beads and one color of 11º seed beads.

1 Add one 10º triangle bead between each bead of a three-bead base or begin with a three-bead base, if starting a new project **a**. Step-up.

2 Add two 10º triangles between each bead **b**. Step-up.

3 Add two 10º triangles at each corner and work peyote for one stitch along each side **c**. Step-up.

4 Add two 10º triangles at each corner and work peyote for two stitches on each side **d**. Step-up.

5 Add **one** 11º seed bead at each corner and work peyote for three stitches on each side using 11º beads. Step-up into the first corner 11º added in this round **e**.

6 Pass through the triangle bead and the first 11º on this side. The shape will start to curve as you work this second side. Work in peyote stitch using 11ºs for two stitches (red) **f**.

7 With the thread exiting the 11º as shown, pick up one 11º (yellow) and pass directly through the first 11º on the next side **g**.

8 Work two 11º peyote stitches (red). Pick up one 11º (yellow) and pass directly into the first 11º bead on the next side **h**.

9 Repeat step 8. To step-up, continue through the (yellow) 11º and the first protruding bead on the next side (red) **i**.

Look closely at the beads at this point and notice that there are two protruding beads on each side, for a total of six beads (the red beads in the picture).

10 Add one 11º between each of the six 11º beads (red beads on the sides and yellow beads on the corners) **j**.

11 Add one 11º bead (orange) between each of the three protruding beads (yellow) to set up a three-bead base for the next section **k**.

a

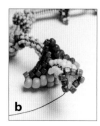
b

c

d

e

f

g

h

i

j

k

DIAMOND STITCH ON a THREE-BEAD BASE

Diamond stitch can be worked on a base of any number of beads. Some examples have already been shown on the rope in the four-bead base sections. This necklace, stitched on a three-bead base, has more examples of how this stitch can be varied using any combination of beads.

DIAMOND STITCH USING BUGLE BEADS

Here, I used a three-bead base consisting of one color of 3mm bugle beads and one color of 11º seed beads.

NOTE: Bugle beads tend to be sharp and can cut the thread. Consider doubling the thread or using a heavier thread (I highly recommend Fireline 8 or even 10 lb. test) to prevent this from happening. Adding a seed bead between bugle beads also helps.

1 Begin from a three-bead base. Pick up one bugle bead, one 11º seed bead, and one bugle. Pass through the next base bead (the three beads added will form a little triangle with the 11º at the top) **a**.

2 Pick up one bugle, one 11º and one bugle. Pass through the next base bead. Pick up one bugle, one 11º, and one bugle. Pass through the last base bead. Step-up by passing through one bugle and the 11º at the top **b**.

3 Pick up one bugle and pass through the next top 11º. Repeat twice. You will not do a step-up here. The thread should be exiting an 11º **c**.

4 Pick up one bugle, one 11º, and one bugle. Pass through the next 11º. Repeat twice.

5 Step-up by passing through one bugle and the top 11º **d**. Easy as that!

On the rope...

Bugle diamond stitch, contrasting color diamond stitch, SuperDuos, Twin beads, 6º, two-hole triangles, and more.

a

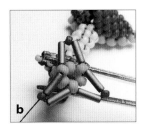

b

c

d

PROJECT
DIAMOND STITCH OPEN-WEAVE NECKLACE

BeaDS

11º seed beads, matte khaki
(color A)
11º seed beads, metallic
bronze (color B)
#3 bugle beads, matte teal
1.5mm cube beads, rose-
lined crystal
3.4mm drop beads, matte
khaki

Bugle beads tend to be sharp and can cut through the thread. See the advice on p. 59. I say this from experience. There is nothing fun about finding a lovingly stitched piece of jewelry all over the floor.

Be sure to leave a long enough tail to create or secure a clasp. I rarely include colors for the beads I use (I like to encourage unique color choice), but for this project I have included them. You're welcome!

1 String three color A 11º seed beads.

2 Pass back through bead 1 to create a circle of beads. The working thread and tail thread will be exiting bead 1 in opposite directions.

3 Pick up two color B 11º seed beads (4 and 5) and pass through bead 2.

4 Pick up two B 11ºs (6 and 7) and pass through bead 3.

5 Pick up two B 11ºs (8 and 9). Pass through bead 1 To finish this round and in order to begin the next round, step-up by passing through bead 4 which is the first bead added in this round.

For this next step, begin to pull the beadwork into a tube shape.

6 With the thread exiting bead 4, pick up one A 11º (10) and pass back down into bead 5. To finish the stitch, pass up into bead 6, as illustrated:

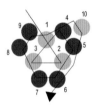

7 With your thread exiting bead 6, pick up one A 11º (11) and pass down into bead 7. To finish the stitch, pass up into bead 8, as illustrated:

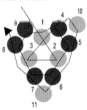

8 With your thread exiting bead 8, pick up one A 11º (12) and pass down into bead 9. To finish the stitch, pass up into bead 4 and step-up into bead 10 as illustrated (red line). Continue gently pulling the beads into the tube/rope shape. Remember, bugle beads can be sharp!

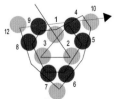

9 Repeat steps 3–8 until the desired length is reached. For instruction purposes, a round of stitching where one bead is added per stitch will be called a "single bead" round, and a round of stitching where two beads are added per stitch will be called a "double bead" round. The necklace here has seven single bead rows before the beads change.

NOTE: The illustrations are drawn flat but the beads are actually pulled into a tube.

This next section uses the bugle beads and the B 11ºs. For illustrative purposes, only the top three A 11ºs from which this next section begins will be shown. These beads are called 1a, 2a, and 3a so there is no confusion with the first beads added in the rope.

10 With your thread exiting bead 1a, pick up two bugle beads, 4a and 5a. Pass through bead 2a to secure.

11 Pick up two bugle beads, 6a and 7a, and pass through bead 3a to secure.

12 Pick up two bugle beads, 8a and 9a, and pass through bead 1a to secure. Step-up into bead 4a to begin the next round.

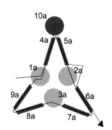

13 Pick up one B 11º and 10a, and pass through bead 5a and back up through bead 6a. Be sure to skip over bead 2a.

14 Add one B 11º (11a) between beads 6a and 7a, skip over bead 3a, pass up through bead 8a, add one B 11º (12a), pass down bead 9a, skip over bead 1a, pass up bead number 4a and step-up into bead 10a to continue the next round. The drawn thread path can be confusing when there are more than two passes of thread through a bead, which is why the old thread passes are eliminated in the illustration.

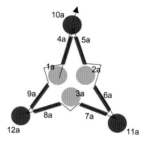

15 Repeat steps 10–14 twice.

16 For the first round of the next section, begin by adding two cube beads per stitch

17 For the second round, add one drop bead between each pair of cube beads.
Rows 3, 5, and 7 are cube beads; rows 4 and 6 are drop beads.

18 Finish this section using one B 11º between each cube bead.
Repeat the bugle bead section.

Feel free to mix it up and create unique patterns using a variety of seed bead sizes, colors and shapes.
Use a shorter length for a great bracelet.

Here is a variation on the same theme.

TOGGLE CLASP

To finish, I hand-stitched a beaded loop and toggle using peyote stitch. Detailed peyote stitch instructions can be found in *Seed Bead Stitching*. The following is an illustration of the toggle loop and basic instructions:

LOOP

1 With the thread exiting the end of the beaded rope, pick up 25 11º seed beads (I used the bronze metallic). Pass through two of the beads from the end of the beaded rope to secure the new beads into a loop.

2 Pick up one 11º and pass through the second of the original 25 beads.

3 Pick up one 11º and pass through the fourth bead as shown.

4 Continue in this manner until the last bead added is secure by passing through the same two end beads from the beaded rope. To continue on to the next round, you will pass through the first bead added in this round.

5 Pick up one drop bead and pass through the next protruding 11º seed bead as illustrated:

6 Continue adding drop bead between the protruding 11ºs in this manner all the way around the loop as illustrated:

Secure the thread for the beaded loop by weaving the thread tail into the beaded rope, tying small knots along the way.

TIP: Before cutting the thread, leave a small loop of thread exposed, apply a swipe of clear nail polish, and then pull the thread loop securely into the beadwork.

BAR

1 Stitch the toggle bar in flat even-count peyote. Begin with 18 11º seed beads on a ¾-yd. length of thread.

2 Pick up one 11º and pass back through the second bead from the end.

3 Pick up one 11º and pass through the fourth bead from the end:

4 Continue adding 11ºs in this manner until the end of the row is reached.

5 Turn and work this peyote stitch until 12 rows are completed.

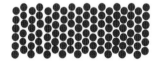

6 To create the beaded tube, roll this flat beadwork into the tube shape and "zip" the two ends together. Weave in the tail threads and secure this toggle bar to the beadwork to complete the necklace/bracelet.

TECHNIQUE
DIAMOND STITCH WITH TWO-HOLE BEADS

On the rope

Twin, SuperDuo, and two-hole triangles. For another idea, use a 6º seed bead instead of the SuperDuo for the single bead round.

quick stitch

This seamlessly connected bangle was created using some of the techniques on the main rope. For a challenge, use SuperDuos or Twin beads, and 11º, 8º, and 6º seed beads (below).

Let's have some fun with SuperDuo, Twin, and two-hole triangle beads.

Begin with a three-bead base **a**.

Add two SuperDuo beads between each base bead for a total of six beads **b**.

To avoid having thread that reaches up to the second hole of the next SuperDuo, I like to reverse the direction of the thread by making a U-turn and passing the needle through the top hole of the same bead the thread is currently exiting **c**.

Pass through the top hole of the next bead **d**.

Add one SuperDuo and pass through the top hole of the next two beads **e**. Repeat twice **f, g**.

To begin the next round, pass through the bottom hole of the first SuperDuo added in this round and U-turn into the top hole of the same bead. The direction of beading will once again change **h**. Add two SuperDuos between each of the three SuperDuos **i**.

NOTE: I added an 11º between pairs of SuperDuos to get ready for a new section.

idea!

a

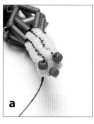
b

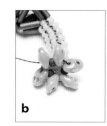
c

d

e

f

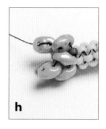
g

h

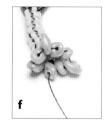
i

three-sided rope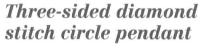

TECHNIQUE
DIAMOND STITCH THREE-SIDED ROPE

 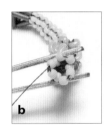

a   **b**   **c**

  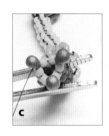

d   **e**   **f**

idea! — *Three-sided diamond stitch circle pendant*

A length of this stitch will easily bend into a circle. To make a seamless connection, end the pattern on round 4 and connect to the first row in the pattern.

On a three-bead base:

Round 1: one 11º between each base bead **a**.

Round 2: two 11ºs between each of the 11º beads **b**.

Round 3: one drop bead within each pair of 11º beads **c**.

Round 4: two 11ºs between each drop bead **d**.

Round 5: one 11º within each pair of 11ºs **e**.

Repeat rounds 2–5 until the desired length is reached **f**.

On the rope...

The three-sided rope is a diamond stitch variation. Use seed beads and drop beads to create a supple rope with three flat sides. Here, I've used 11ºs with 3.4mm drops.

Beads

11º seed beads

SuperDuo

Two-hole triangle

Twin

Rulla

TECHNIQUE
ZEN GARDEN ON A THREE-BEAD BASE

Three-bead zen garden is created the same way as shown on p. 28. The difference is there will be three two-hole beads per round instead of two. The direction of the beading will change each row in order to create the offset design.

1 Beginning with a three-bead base, add two 11º beads between each base bead **a**.

2 With the thread exiting the first bead of a bead pair, pick up one SuperDuo bead. Pass down through the second hole of the SuperDuo and through the second bead of the 11º bead pair. Immediately pass up into the first bead of the next 11º bead pair **b**.

3 Add two more SuperDuos in the same manner as in Step 2. Step-up by passing up into the first hole of the first SuperDuo added in this round **c**.

4 To create the zen pattern, change the stitching direction for this round. With the thread exiting one of the holes of the SuperDuo, pick up one SuperDuo bead. Pass down through the second hole of the SuperDuo bead and the first hole of the adjacent SuperDuo, making sure that the newly added SuperDuo sits between the two SuperDuos of the previous round.

Pass up into the second hole of the SuperDuo **d**.

a

b

c

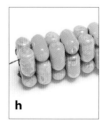

d

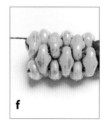

e

f

g

h

On the rope

Zen garden with SuperDuo, two-hole triangles, Twin beads, and Rulla beads. Wow! Using Rulla beads did NOT turn out as expected. It turned out better! As I was creating the central rope, I already knew how the Twin, SuperDuo and two-hole triangle beads would look, but I had never tried using Rulla beads for the three-bead base, only for the four-bead base. I am so excited to have discovered another stacking technique I will refer to as zen Rulla.

And now I have another idea, but I have to keep moving on this rope. In the meantime, try this project that combines zen garden with puffy triangles.

5 Add two more SuperDuos in the same manner as in Step 4. Step-up into the first hole of the first SuperDuo added in this round **e**.

6 Change direction once again to continue the zen pattern of beads until the desired length is reached **f**.

Try using other two-hole beads such as the two-hole triangles **g** and Rullas **h**.

zen Triangle Necklace

This fabulous necklace incorporates the three-bead zen garden technique with the puffy triangle technique.

Alternate 10 rows of zen garden using Twin beads, with puffy triangles using 6º seed beads. Add 11º seed beads on either side of the puffy triangles.

captured pearls

Beads

11º seed beads

8º seed beads

6mm round gemstones or pearls

CAPTURED BEAD NETTING

This netting stitch uses 11º and 8º seed beads to capture 6mm rounds right in the stitch.

1 On a three-bead base, add one 8º seed bead between each base bead and step-up into the first 8º added **a**.

2 With the thread exiting the 8º, pick up three 11º seed beads, one 8º, and three 11ºs. Pass through the next 8º **b**.

3 Repeat step 2 **c**. Repeat again, and step-up by passing through the first three 11ºs and the 8º **d**.

4 With the thread exiting the 8º, pick up one 6mm gemstone and pass through the next 8º only. Do not pass through any of the 11ºs **e**.

5 Add a 6mm, securing through the next 8º, again without passing thorough any of the 11ºs **f**.

6 Add a 6mm, securing through the next 8º, which is the same bead that began this round **g**. (There is no step-up into the first bead added. The round always begins with the thread exiting the 8º.)

7 Repeat steps 3–6 a few times.

8 To end a section of captured stone netting, pick up the three 8ºs and circle through the beads a couple of times to tighten **h**.

There is now a new three-bead base from which to start a new section of beadwork.

a

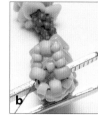

b

c

d

e

f

g

h

NETTING BRACELET WITH PUFFY TRIANGLE CORNERS

This fun project combines the captured stone netting technique (using 11º seed beads, 8º seed beads, and 6mm Swarovski pearls) with the puffy triangle technique. I like the size consistency of the faux pearls for this technique. The captured stone and the puffy triangle techniques have each been explained in detail. These instructions should be easy to follow.

1 Beginning with a three-bead base of 11º seed beads, add two beads in between each base bead for a total of six beads.

2 Add one 11º within each pair of beads added in the last round for a total of three beads.

3 Add one 8º seed bead between each 11º for a total of three beads.

4 Create a puffy triangle using 8ºs. When there are five rows complete (count the rows on the diagonal from the center 8º) begin the decrease of the triangle. There will be three 8ºs ready to be used as the base for the next section.

5 Add two 11ºs between each 8º for a total of six beads.

6 Add one 11º within each pair of beads added in the last round, for a total of three beads.

7 Add one 8º between each 11º for a total of three beads.

8 Pick up three 11ºs, one 8º and three 11ºs. Secure by passing through the next 8º from the previous round.

9 Follow the instructions for the captured stone netting technique until there are the desired number of rows of pearls.

10 The captured stone netting technique will end with three 8ºs, which are the base for the next section.

11 Add one 11º between each 8º for a total of three beads.

12 Add two 11ºs between each 11º for a total of six beads.

13 Add one 11º within each pair of beads added in the previous round for a total of three beads.

14 Add one 8º between each 11º and begin the next puffy triangle.

15 Continue working, alternating the techniques until there are four netting sections and four triangles.

16 After completing the last netting section, add one 11º between each 8º, and then add two beads between each of those beads. The bracelet can now be seamlessly connected using the first three base beads from Step 1.

Another bead, another look

This bracelet uses 11º beads, 8º beads, and six rows of 6mm gemstone beads. It fits my 6-in. wrist (8 in. around the largest part of my hand).

mushroom

TECHNIQUE
FOLDED TRIANGLE TWO WAYS

This technique just appeared one day and I loved it! The best part about it is that it can be folded two ways for two completely different looks!

MUSHROOM FOLD

1 Begin on a three-bead base Add two 11º seed beads between each base bead.

2 Using 11ºs, work two rounds for the start of a puffy triangle **a** (p. 54) .

3 Using 8º seed beads, grow the triangle for two more rounds **b** .

NOTE: the triangle will start to wave because the 8ºs are larger than the 11ºs.

4 Using 6º seed beads, grow the triangle for another round, but instead of picking up two 6ºs at each corner, pick up one 6º, one 8º, and one 6º **c**.

5 With the thread exiting the first corner bead, weave around the outside of the triangle until the thread is exiting the center bead on one of the sides **d**.

6 With the thread exiting the center bead, pass through the center beads on the next side and the center bead on the last side. The triangle will fold onto itself **e**, **f**.

FOLDED TRIANGLE BRACELET

Using the folded triangle techniques, diamond stitch using Twin and/or SuperDuo beads, puffy triangle, or any techniques that have been covered, create a one-of-a-kind bracelet.

a   b   c   d   e   f

three circle

Weave through these three beads again to tighten the beads and to set up for the next section.

THREE CIRCLE FOLD

Create a triangle as in mushroom fold using 11º seed beads for two rounds, 8º seed beads for three rounds, and 6º seed beads for two rounds. Make sure to add an 8º between the 6º corner pair on the last round. After completing the last stitch, pass through the corner 8º to position for the fold.

To fold this triangle, pass through the 8ºs on each corner. Pass through all three beads again. It may take a little finessing to get the beads to curve in the right direction. Be gentle so as not to break the thread.

THREE CIRCLE FOLD PENDANT

Create a pendant using the folded triangle three-sided version, a peyote saucer, puffy triangle, and diamond stitch. Make sure to step-up at the end of each round.

Begin this pendant with the three-circle folded triangle. Leave plenty of tail thread to be able to create a peyote saucer on the underside of the folded triangle.

1 Create of circle of beads using 15º seed beads.

2 Work three rounds as described in the folded triangle instructions using the 15ºs.

3 Work two rounds using 11º seed beads.

4 Work two rounds using 1.5 or 1.8 mm cube beads.

5 Work one round using 8º Delica beads.

6 Work one round using 6º seed beads. Use only one 6º at each corner.

7 Create the three-circle form by stitching through the three corner beads. Circle through them again to tighten and hold in place **a**, **b** (side view).

8 Add one 8º between each of the three beads of the folded triangle.

9 Create a puffy triangle using the same 8ºs as in step 8. Work for three rounds and then begin the decrease.

10 Refer to photo **c** for steps 10–27. Add one 1.5 or 1/8mm cube bead between each of the three beads of the puffy triangle.

11 Working in diamond stitch, add two cubes between each of the cubes from Step 10.

12 Add one 15º within each cube pair.

13 Add two cubes between each 15º.

14 Add one cube within each cube pair.

This next section is created using a variation of the diamond stitch.

15 Add one 6º seed bead between each cube.

a

b

c

16 Add two 11ºs between each 6º. Step-up into the first bead of the first pair added in the round.

17 Pick up one 11º and pass through the second bead of the 11º pair, the 6º and the first bead of the next 11º pair.

18 Pick up one 11º and pass through the second bead of the 11º pair, the 6º, and the first bead of the next 11º pair.

19 Pick up one 11º and pass through the second bead of the 11º pair, the 6º, and the first bead of the next 11º pair. Step-up into the first bead added in this round.

20 Pick up three 11ºs and pass into the single 11º on the other side of the 6º.

21 Pick up three 11ºs and pass into the single 11º on the other side of the 6º bead.

22 Pick up three 11ºs and pass into the single 11º on the other side of the 6º bead. Pass through the first two beads of the first three-bead set added in this round.

23 Pick up one 6º and pass through the center bead of the next three-bead set added in the previous round.

play!

24 Pick up one 6º and pass through the center bead of the next three-bead set added in the previous round.

25 Pick up one 6º and pass through the center bead of the next three-bead set added in the previous round. Step-up into the first 6º added in this round.

26 Repeat steps 16–22.

27 Repeat steps 23–25 using 8ºs instead of the 6ºs.

28 Create a loop to finish.

29 Using the long tail thread as suggested at the beginning of the instructions, create a peyote ball or saucer underneath the folded triangle. Find instructions for the three-bead peyote ball on p. 48, and the peyote saucer on p. 47.

11's and 8's

idea! Use three different beads changing bead placement every few rows as in the bracelet below.

PROJECT
DO THE TWIST
a BOBBE STITCH VaRIaTION

Use one small bead together with one large bead: 11º seed beads and 8º seed beads or 15º seed beads and 11º seed beads. Work from a three-bead base, either new or from a previous round.

1 Add one 11º seed bead and one 8º seed bead between each of the three beads in the base row (three pairs of beads). Step-up into the first 11º added in this round **a**.

2 Pick up one 11º and pass through the first bead of the next pair of beads (the 11º). Repeat twice. Step-up into the first 11º added in this round **a**.

3 Repeat steps 1 and 2 until the desired length is reached. The twist will appear after a few rounds **c**.

NOTE: Be sure to keep the 8º seed beads to the outside of the twisted shape. The thread tends to wrap around them.

a

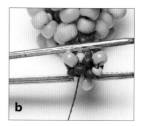

b

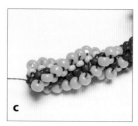

c

Beads

PROJECT
TWIST & GOLD NECKLACE

The structure and techniques of this necklace should be very recognizable by now.

1 Begin with a seven-row puffy triangle using 11º seed beads.

2 Add one round of 11ºs to separate the next technique.

3 Stitch a peyote ball (p. 38).

4 Stitch 60 rows of do the twist.

5 Add one round of 11ºs to separate the next technique.

6 Repeat step 3.

7 Stitch a diamond stitch section using 15º seed beads for the bead pairs and 11ºs for the single bead round.

8 Repeat steps 2–7 to create the second side of the necklace. This necklace is finished with my signature fan toggle and beaded loop.

TWIST & DIAMOND NECKLACE

1 Stitch a five-row puffy triangle using 11º seed beads.

2 Add a five-round peyote ball.

3 Alternate techniques until there are three puffy triangles and two peyote balls.

4 Work diamond stitch for 16 patterns using 11ºs for the pairs and 8º seed beads for the singles.

5 Stitch three peyote balls using 11ºs. Separate the balls with a single round of tubular peyote.

6 Stitch Do The Twist for 52 rows.

7 Repeat steps 1–6 for the desired length.

8 Finish with a clasp or a seamless closure.

On the rope

To add more pizazz, I tried the twist using three color combinations. After ripping it out a few times, I figured out the pattern I was hoping for. Here it is:

Round 1:
First stitch, cube A and long drop A. Second stitch, 11º B and Rizo B. Third stitch, 11º C and Rizo C. Step-up.

Round 2:
First stitch, 11º B. Second stitch, 11º C. Third stitch, cube bead A. Step-up.

Round 3:
First stitch 11º B and Rizo B. Second stitch, 11º C and Rizo C. Third stitch, Cube bead A and long drop.

Round 4:
First stitch 11º C. Second stitch, Cube A. Third stitch, 11º B.

Round 5:
First stitch 11º C and Rizo C. Second stitch, Cube bead A and long drop. Third stitch, 11º B and Rizo B.

Round 6:
First stitch Cube A. Second stitch, 11º B. Third stitch, 11º C.

Repeat rounds 1–6 for the desired length.

TECHNIQUE
TRELLIS PATTERN

While many of my techniques have unlimited variations created just by changing the type or order of the beads, this pattern is not one of those. Trellis pattern is created by specific bead color placement. Create variations by using different size beads. I think it looks best with two contrasting colors of the same size bead, but feel free to play.

Using two colors, A and B, this pattern repeats every four rows.

1 Begin with three A beads. If this is the beginning of a new project, create a circle of the As **a**.

2 Add one B bead between each of the three As **b**. Step-up.

3 Add two beads in B–A order between each of the Bs **c**. Step-up.

4 Add two As, securing into the B only of each pair from the previous round **d**. Step-up.

5 Add one B within each pair of As (**e**, **f**). Step-up.

6 Repeat steps 3–5 until the desired length is reached **g**. This pattern can be created on a three-bead or four-bead base. See the *Jester Lariat* in the gallery (p. 94) for a colorful way to use this pattern.

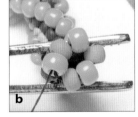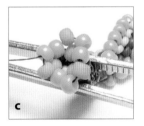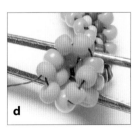

giant ruffle

Beads

TECHNIQUE
GIANT RUFFLE

I have no idea which part of my brain thought this up, but anyone who has followed my work will know that at one time I loved to play with ruffles. Although this is different than my past work, it still takes me back.

NOTE: For purpose of instruction, this technique is made on a three-bead base, which turns into a six-bead base in step 1. I have not tried a four-bead base (that does NOT turn into an eight-bead base), but it would be thinner due to having two less columns of beads to ruffle.

1 Add two color A 8º seed beads between each of three base beads for a total of six beads. Step-up.

2 Stitch the next round in tubular herringbone using color A 11º seed beads **a**. Step-up.

3 Stitch the next round in tubular herringbone using A 8ºs **b**.

a

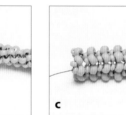

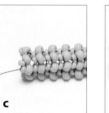

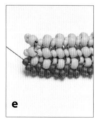

b

c

d

e

f

g

h

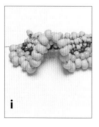
i

j

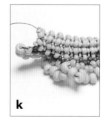
k

4 Continue working in tubular herringbone alternating the rows using 11ºs and 8ºs. Create any length section, but end with an 11º **c**.

Let the ruffles begin! Look at the section just created. The ruffles will be created along the rope on every other bead column, not AROUND the circumference of the rope. After creating the first ruffle, you'll skip over a bead column and begin the second ruffle, but we are not at that point yet.

5 With the thread exiting the A 11º, pick up one B 11º, turn, and pass through the first A 8º in the column. Work flat peyote along the column, making sure to pass into each A 8º after picking up a B 11º **d**.

6 With the thread exiting the last A 8º, pick up two B 11º s, turn, and pass through the first B 11º. Work peyote again along the entire length of the column using two B 11ºs per stitch, making sure to pass through each B 11º added in the previous step **e**.

7 Pick up one C 8º, turn and work peyote along the length passing through the pairs of B 11ºs added in the last step. The shape will start to ruffle **f**.

8 Pick up two C 8ºs, turn, and work peyote again to the end **g**. Notice that the ruffle is forming.

9 Pick up one 6º seed bead, turn, and work peyote to the end, making sure to pass through each pair of 8ºs from the previous step **h**.

10 Pick up two 6ºs, turn, and work peyote to the end **i**.

Notice that the thread is exiting from a 6º. Pass down through the adjacent 8º, up into the adjacent 11º, down through the 11º and 8º adjacent beads, and up into the adjacent 8º and 11º beads. This will position thread for the beginning of the next ruffle. Remember that the ruffles are made on every other column of beads **j**, **k**.

11 Create a second ruffle following steps 5–10.

12 Create a third ruffle following steps 5–10.

NOTE: I'm using the simple transition as described on p. 44. Add two beads between each of the three base beads. Pick up one bead and pass through three beads. Pick up one bead and pass through three beads. Step-up into the first of the two beads added in this round. Add two beads between each of the two beads. Step-up into the first bead added. This is now a base for skinny herringbone. Easy!

BEADS

Skinny Herringbone:

15º seed beads

Graduated Pattern Sections:

11º seed beads

1.5mm (or 1.8 mm) cube beads

8º seed beads

6º seed beads

PROJECT
GRADUATED BOBBE/ HERRINGBONE VARIATIONS

These necklaces (below and p. 81) are all made on a four-bead skinny tubular herringbone base, which separates the graduated Bobbe Stitch patterns.

1 Stitch 10–15 rows of skinny herringbone using 15º seed beads. With the thread exiting the first bead of a bead pair in the skinny herringbone section, pick up one 11º seed bead, pass down through the second bead of the pair, and up into the first bead of the next pair. Pick up one 11º and pass down through the second bead of the pair. Pass up into the first bead of the first pair to finish the stitch and step-up into the first 11º added in this round **a**.

2 Pick up two 11ºs and pass through the opposite 11º to secure **b**.

3 Pick up two 11ºs and pass through the 11º at the start of the round. Step-up into the first bead of the first pair **c.**

4 With the thread exiting the first bead of the 11º pair, pick up two 11ºs. Following the instructions for Bobbe

stitch, don't pass down into the second bead of the bead pair, but instead pass up directly into the first bead of the next bead pair **d.**

5 Pick up two 11ºs. Don't pass down into the second bead of the pair, but instead pass directly up into the first bead of the first pair. Step-up into the first bead of the first pair added in this round **e.**

6 Pick up one cube bead. Don't pass down into the second bead of the pair, but instead pass directly up into the first bead of the next pair **f**. Repeat one more time for this round **g**. Step-up into the first bead added in this step.

7 Repeat steps 3–5 using cube beads.

8 Repeat step 6 using an 8º seed bead.

9 Repeat steps 3–5 using 8ºs.

10 Repeat step 6 using a 6º seed bead.

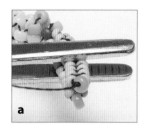 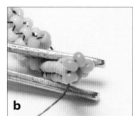 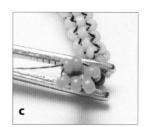 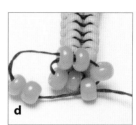

a **b** **c** **d**

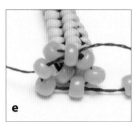  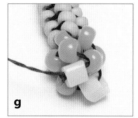

e **f** **g**

11 Repeat steps 3–5 using 6ºs.

12 Repeat step 6 using a 6º. Don't miss this! It keeps the pattern symmetrical.

13 Repeat steps 3–5 using 8ºs.

14 Repeat step 6 using an 8ºs.

15 Repeat steps 3–5 using cube beads.

16 Repeat step 6 using cube beads.

17 Repeat steps 3–5 using 11ºs.

18 Repeat step 6 using 11ºs.

19 With the thread exiting an 11º, begin a new skinny herringbone section using the two beads just added in step 19.

Continue working in this manner until the desired length is reached.

idea!

Instead of beginning by adding one 11º within a bead-base pair (for a total of two beads added), add one 11º between each of the four beads on the skinny herringbone base (for a total of four beads added in the round). The necklace is worked like the other three, but with four stitches per round instead of two, which creates a fatter bobbe section (as seen on the rope, above). This can also be done on a three-bead base.

HERRINGBONE WITH SPIRAL BOBBE

1 Begin with several rows of skinny herringbone stitch.

2 To create the spiral, with the thread exiting the first bead of a bead pair, pick up one 11º seed bead and one drop bead or top-drilled pearl, and pass directly up into the first bead of the next pair **a**.

Repeat, making sure to step-up into the first 11º added in this step **b**.

NOTE: For each of the spiral rows, pass through only the 11ºs in each bead pair. This is the first bead of each pair.

3 Repeat step 2 for several rounds.

4 To end the spiral, pick up two 11ºs and pass directly through the opposite 11º. Repeat one more time and step-up into the first bead added in this step **c**. To vary this technique, use two different beads for the second beads of each pair, i.e. a drop bead for one stitch and a triangle bead for the other stitch. Or just use a drop bead for one stitch in each round.

Experiment with different bead combinations. It's all about the "Play!"

On the rope

Spiral bobbe with 11º seed bead and long drop. Spiral bobbe with 11º seed beads and long magatamas for one stitch and spiral bobbe with 11º seed beads and 11º triangle beads for the other stitch. Spiral bobbe with 11º seed beads and SuperUnos for one stitch and 11º sharp triangle beads with Rizo beads for the other stitch.

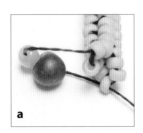

a

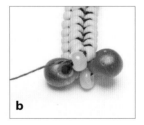

b

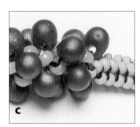

c

TECHNIQUE
SIMPLE SKINNY TUBULAR HERRINGBONE TWIST

To create this easy twist, use two different size beads, like the 8º seed beads and 6º seed beads shown here, for each skinny tubular herringbone stitch. Keep the order of the beads the same throughout.

On the rope
Finish the rope by using skinny herringbone and a fan toggle. Tah Dah!

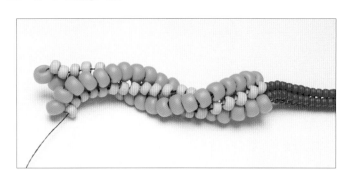

PROJECT
BERRIES FOR BREAKFAST

My friend Marlene Quigley asked me to recreate, in seed beads, her stone and glass bead design. I quickly designed section 1 and liked it so much that I decided to keep working using different stitching techniques. Before long, this necklace was finished.

NOTE: There is no right or wrong way to make this necklace. Each component can be put in different places, or can be varied. It's all about the "bead play." Experiment and see where it takes you. These instructions begin at the center of the necklace and work outward. When you get to the end, you can use any type of clasp or closure that you like. The toggle shown here is my signature design.

As you work, remember to step-up after each round.

SECTION 1 (CENTERPIECE)

1 Begin with 15 rows of skinny her-ringbone using a base of four 15º seed beads. Be very careful NOT to split the thread when beginning because the initial row of thread will be removed. NOT the beads, just the thread.

2 Add one 11º seed bead (red in the illustration) between each of the four 15ºs. Step-up.

3 Add two 11ºs between each of the four 11ºs just added. Step-up into the first bead of the first pair added in the round.

4 Pick-up one 11º. Pass through the second of the pair and the first of the next pair. Repeat three more times, stepping up into the first bead added in the round. At this point, start pulling the beads into a tube shape.

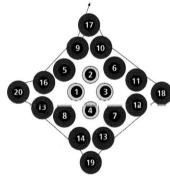

5 Add two 11ºs between each 11º. Step-up into the first bead of the first p

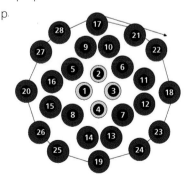

NOTE: The next diagram shows only the pairs and the four new beads that will be added in this new round.

Pick-up one 11º, pass through the second bead of the pair, and up into the first bead of the next pair. Repeat three more times. Step-up into the first bead added in this round.

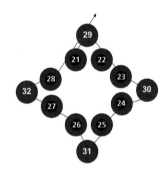

6 Add one 8º seed bead (silver/gray) between each of the 11ºs added in the previous round. Step-up.

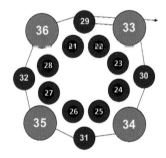

Add two 8ºs between each of the four beads. Step-up.

Step-up at the end of each round!

Add one 8º between each of the eight beads added.

Add one 8º between each of the eight beads again.

Pick up one 8º and pass through the next two 8ºs. Repeat three more times.

(The next section is turquoise.)

Add one 8º between each 8º from the previous round.

Add two 8ºs between each 8º.

Add one 8º between each 8º.

Add one 8º between each 8º again

Add one 6º seed bead between each 8º.

Add one 8º between each 6º.

Add one 8º between each 8º.

Add one 8º between each 8º again.

Add one 8º and pass through two 8ºs. Repeat three more times.

(Back to silver/gray bead as shown in the picture.)

Add one 8º (silver/gray) between each 8º (turquoise) for a total of four beads.

Add two beads between each bead added in the last round.

Add one bead between each of the eight beads just added.

Add one bead between each of the eight beads again

Add one bead and pass through the next two beads. Repeat three more times.

(Back to the reddish beads as shown in the picture.)

Add one bead between each of the four silvery beads

Add two beads between each bead.

Add one bead between each pair.

Add two beads between each bead.

Add one bead between each pair.

(Back to the 15ºs.)

Add one 15º between each reddish bead (total of four).

Work skinny herringbone for 15 rows.

SECTION 2 THREE BABY BERRIES

You learned this stitch as peyote bumps. These beads are turquoise in the picture.

*Add one 11º between each of the 15ºs.

Add one 8º between each of the 11ºs.

Add one 6º between each of the 8ºs.

Add one 8º between each of the 6ºs.

Add one 11º between each of the 8ºs.

Switch to the 15ºs**.

Add one 15º between each of the 11ºs from the previous round.

Add two 15ºs between each of the 15ºs.

Add one 15º between each pair or 15ºs from the previous round***.

Repeat from * to ***.

Repeat from * to **.

Using the 15ºs, work skinny herringbone for 15 rows.

SECTION 3 BERRY HUG

You learned this stitch as peyote saucers.

*Add one 11º (red) between each 15º.

Add one 11º between each 11º added in the previous round.

Add two 11ºs between each 11º.

Add one 11º between EACH bead in the previous round for a total of eight beads.

Add two 11ºs between each of the eight beads for a total of 16 beads in this round (eight pair of beads).

With your thread exiting one of the beads of a bead pair, pick up one 11º, pass through the second bead of the pair, and immediately pass into the first bead of the next pair.

Add two 11ºs between each bead from the previous round.

With your thread exiting the first bead of a bead pair, pick up one 11º, pass through the second bead of the pair, and immediately pass into the first bead of the next pair.

Add one 11º between each bead from the last round.

Pick up one 11º. Pass through the next two beads. Repeat three more times. You will have added four beads in this round.

Add one 11º between each of the 11ºs from the previous round.**

Add one silver/gray 8º between each red 11º.

Add two silver/gray 8ºs between each 8º.

With your thread exiting the first bead of the bead pair, pick up one bead, pass through the second bead of the bead pair, and immediately pass into the first bead of the next pair. Repeat three times.

Using the red 11ºs, repeat from * to **.

Add one 15º bead between each of the four red 11ºs. Work skinny herring bone for fifteen rows.

SECTION 4 BERRY POD

You learned this stitch as diamond stitch variation.

Add one turquoise 11º between each of the four 15ºs.

Add two turquoise 11ºs between each of the 11ºs.

With your thread exiting the first bead of bead pair, pick up one turquoise 11º, pass through the second bead of the pair, and immediately pas up into the first bead of the next pair. Repeat three more times.

Add two turquoise 8ºs between each of the four 8ºs from the previous round.

With your thread exiting the first bead of bead pair, pick up one turquoise 8º, pass through the second bead of the pair, and immediately pass up into the first bead of the next pair. Repeat three more times.

Add two turquoise 6ºs between each of the four 8ºs.

With your thread exiting the first bead of bead pair, pick up one turquoise

6º, pass through the second bead of the pair, and immediately pass up into the first bead of the next pair. Repeat three more times.

Add two 6ºs between each of the four 6ºs from the previous round.

With your thread exiting the first bead of bead pair, pick up one turquoise 8º, pass through the second bead of the pair, and immediately pass up into the first bead of the next pair. Repeat three more times.

Add two 8ºs between each of the four 8ºs from the previous round.

With your thread exiting the first bead of bead pair, pick up one turquoise 11º, pass through the second bead of the pair, and immediately pass up into the first bead of the next pair. Repeat three more times.

Add two 11ºs between each of the four 11ºs added in the previous round.

With your thread exiting the first bead of the bead pair, pick up one turquoise 11º, pass through the second bead of the pair, and immediately pass up into the first bead of the next pair. Repeat three more times.

Add one 15º between each of the four 11ºs added in the previous round.

Work skinny herringbone for 15 rows.

SECTION 5 THREE BABY BERRIES VARIATION

You learned this stitch as peyote bumps.

Using the section 2 instructions, use a red 11º instead of the turquoise 11º, the silver/gray 8º instead of the turquoise 8º, and the turquoise 6º as directed.

Add one 15º in between each of the 11ºs.

Work skinny herringbone for 15 rows.

BERRY POD

You learned this stitch as diamond stitch variation. Repeat the section 4 instructions.

Add one 15º between each of the turquoise 11ºs from the last round of the berry pod.

Work skinny herringbone for 15 rows.

You have now completed one half of the necklace. To continue working the other side, carefully remove the first round of thread. Your thread should be exiting the middle of a pair of beads.

Add one turquoise 11º to begin the first section of "three baby berries."

Follow the instructions for each section until you have reached the end.

PROJECT
CIRCLE PENDANT

All of the components used in this project have been described and illustrated earlier. Use the design idea presented here as inspiration for a new unique pendant.

Create an embellished circle as in Circle Game, p. 16. Embellish as much as desired using several rows of beads for the outer circles to create a circle of any size.

Using one of the edge beads, create a two-bead base to begin a section of harlequin diamond.

Create a peyote saucer.

Create a bail as described in S Pendant, p. 31.

PROJECT
PIGGY CIRCLE PENDANT

The idea for Piggy Circle Pendant came to me when I had no idea what to do with the beads that have a cupped shape with two holes, one in the center and one off-center, and just started playing.

Begin with a herringbone circle as described in Circle Game, p. 16, using 11º and 8º seed beads.

Use the same 11ºs for the first embellishment round. Make sure to step-up into the first 11º added in this round.

Use one hole of a Twin bead for the next embellishment round, making sure to step-up into the bottom hole of the first Twin bead added in the round.

After completing the Twin round, it is necessary to position for the next round. With the thread exiting the bottom hole of the first Twin bead added in this round, make a U-turn and pass through the top hole of the same bead. The direction of beading will change for this round. Add one 8º between

each top hole of the Twin beads. In other words, if the Twin beads were added in a clockwise direction, this round of beads will be added in a counterclockwise direction or vice versa. Step-up into the first 8º added in this round.

Continuing in the same direction, use one 11º and one piggy bead (using the offset hole) for each stitch. At the end of this round, step-up by passing through the first 11º and the first piggy beads added in the round.

To complete the last round, the direction will once again change. With the thread exiting the offset hole of the piggy bead, make a U-turn and pass though the center hole of the same piggy bead. Add 6º seed beads between each of the piggy beads using the center holes of the piggy beads.

Create a loop in the back of the pendant for a neck chain.

PROJECT
LONG SIMPLE PENDANTS

Using several stitching techniques, create a short rope, add a beaded bail, and suspend it from your favorite neck strap or cable.

This is not really a project because I am not going to describe it stitch-by-stitch or row-by-row. My goal has always been to teach techniques to beaders who will then take what they have learned to find a way to give it their own spin. I like the sleek look of this necklace. Look at this and allow it to inspire something unique, fun, and playful. This book is called *Bead Play Every Day* for a reason!

PROJECT
SLEEK COLOR-BLOCKING NECKLACE

*Gallery

Bead soup Bobbe Stitch necklace with Large Peyote Saucer Stitch variation

Zen Garden, Diamond Stitch, and Herringbone bangle

Skinny Herringbone with Spiral Bobbe Stitch, Peyote Ball, and Diamond Stitch Ball

Bobbe Stitch using daggers for dramatic texture

Peyote Balls and Peyote Saucer ring

Skinny Herringbone Stitch flanks a Large Peyote Ball (6º beads)

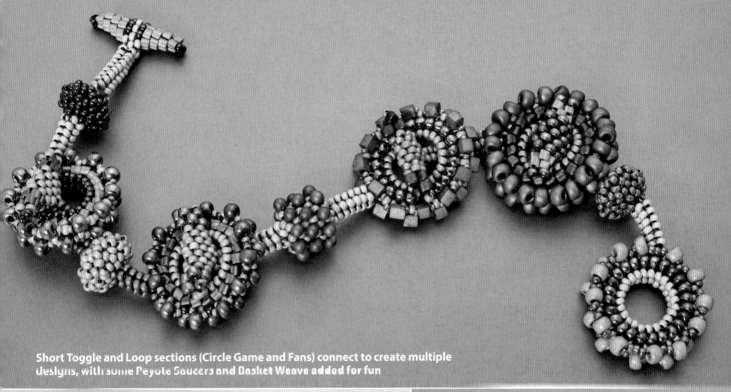

Short Toggle and Loop sections (Circle Game and Fans) connect to create multiple designs, with some Peyote Saucers and Basket Weave added for fun

"Cocoa Berries" necklace adapted from "Berries for Breakfast" (p. 84)

"Black and White in Color" bangle using many techniques

Captured Stone Netting using Swarovski pearls and spike beads, surrounded by Puffy Triangles and Peyote Saucers

A bracelet of Peyote Saucers created with a variety of beads

Jester Lariat highlighting Trellis Pattern, Peyote Saucers, Peyote Ruffle, Harlequin Diamond, and Diamond Stitch; stitched using "Herringbone with a Flair."

CONCLUSION

I hope you enjoyed this book and another glimpse into the evolution of my work and more about what makes me so passionate about this art. And, I hope you have time for some final thoughts that are more spiritually profound for me.

INSPIRATION POINT

While hiking to Inspiration Point in Phoenix, Ariz., several years ago, I was forced to look down at certain times to make sure that I did not trip. As I was watching my feet, I couldn't help but notice that my footprints were covering many others as I made my way up the mountain. This struck me profoundly as I thought about my bead journey and about the beaders, like hikers, who have come before me; and the beaders, like hikers, who will come along after me. I realized that as artists, we all leave our own footprints along the way. Over time our footprints may disappear, but the fact that they were once there is what matters.

Beading is an art that will carry on through time because of the people who have dared to climb the mountain by learning, creating, designing, teaching, and sharing.

I thank those who have forged the trail and I thank those who trust the trail enough to add their own footprints. And today, I thank those who trust me enough to join me as I work to forge my own trail.

This is beauty. This is art.

THE APPALACHIAN TRAIL

While my thoughts about Inspiration Point still ring true, I found myself adding to them while on a recent hike on the Appalachian trail, with my always-supportive husband, in the Blue Ridge Mountains in northern Georgia. The trail was difficult, strenuous, all uphill, and full of slippery rocks that tested our endurance and balance for the better part of an hour. We were told that at a certain point on this trail, we would turn off onto another trail where the terrain would be grassy and easier to maneuver, and that we would come to a lookout with a view like no other. As we made our way, we found both of these things to be true. As we sat down for lunch overlooking a most spectacular landscape, I realized that the trail and beautiful overlook mirrored the last several years of my beading career. While there is no question that I am passionate about beads and always have been, I had somehow lost my creative spark and found a "rocky climb" back to what has become my own personal "beautiful overlook" in this book you are holding.

The hike, and a dream about a beaded necklace, rekindled my beading passion. Needless to say, I'm so happy to be back!

The next time you take a walk, look down and think about those who have walked the same path toward their own goals.

Thank you for joining me on this new journey. I hope you found inspiration and I hope you find a moment to leave your own footprints on the trail.

 With love, Beth

Beth Stone has a passion for beads and a creative, inquisitive approach to stitching with them. She was first published in Bead&Button *magazine in 1998 and since then, has been featured numerous times in magazines and books, including writing her own:* Seed Bead Stitching, *and* More Seed Bead Stitching. *She lives in West Bloomfield, Mich., with her husband, daughters, and dog. She loves the dialog that sharing her bead artistry has opened, so please contact Beth via e-mail at bnshdl@msn.com or visit her Facebook page,* Bead-Play-Every-Day.